T0354868

WRECKLESS
IN THE CITY

WRECKLESS
IN THE CITY

Physics of Safe Driving for Teenage Drivers
(and adults too)

DEJI BADIRU

WRECKLESS IN THE CITY
PHYSICS OF SAFE DRIVING FOR TEENAGE DRIVERS
(AND ADULTS TOO)

iUniverse books may be ordered through booksellers or by contacting:

iUniverse
1663 Liberty Drive
Bloomington, IN 47403
www.iuniverse.com
844-349-9409

Because of the dynamic nature of the Internet, any web addresses or links contained in this book may have changed since publication and may no longer be valid. The views expressed in this work are solely those of the author and do not necessarily reflect the views of the publisher, and the publisher hereby disclaims any responsibility for them.

Any people depicted in stock imagery provided by Getty Images are models, and such images are being used for illustrative purposes only.
Certain stock imagery © Getty Images.

Cover Illustration Credit: Kaffy Taiwo Rasheed, Kaffy Studio, Lagos, Nigeria

ISBN: 978-1-6632-6359-9 (sc)
ISBN: 978-1-6632-6360-5 (e)

Library of Congress Control Number: 2024911066

Print information available on the last page.

iUniverse rev. date: 05/31/2024

ABICS Publications
A Division of
AB International Consulting Services

Books in the ABICS Publications Book Series
(www.abicspublications.com)

1. **Wreckless in the City: Physics of Safe Driving for teenage drivers (and adults too),** iUniverse, Bloomington, Indiana, 2024.
2. **Margin of Death: How close we come each day,** iUniverse, Bloomington, Indiana, 2024
3. **Soccer Greatness at Saint Finbarr's College (Volume II): Legacy of All-Around Sports,** iUniverse, Bloomington, Indiana, 2024
4. **Academics, Discipline, and Sports at Saint Finbarr's College: Tributes to the Great Soccer Players,** iUniverse, Bloomington, Indiana, 2023.
5. **More Physics of Soccer: Playing the Game Smart and Safe,** iUniverse, Bloomington, Indiana, 2022.
6. **Rapidity: Time Management on the Dot,** iUniverse, Bloomington, Indiana, 2022.
7. **The Physics of Skateboarding: Fun, Fellowship, and Following,** iUniverse, Bloomington, Indiana, 2021.
8. **My Everlasting Education at Saint Finbarr's College: Academics, Discipline, and Sports,** iUniverse, Bloomington, Indiana, 2020.
9. **Twenty-Fifth Hour: Secrets to Getting More Done Every Day,** iUniverse, Bloomington, Indiana, 2020.
10. **Kitchen Project Management: The Art and Science of an Organized Kitchen,** iUniverse, Bloomington, Indiana, 2020.
11. **Wives of the Same School: Tributes and Straight Talk,** iUniverse, Bloomington, Indiana, 2019.

12. **The Rooster and the Hen: The Story of Love at Last Look**, iUniverse, Bloomington, Indiana, 2018.

13. **Kitchen Physics: Dynamic Nigerian Recipes**, iUniverse, Bloomington, Indiana, 2018.

14. **The Story of Saint Finbarr's College: Father Slattery's Contributions to Education and Sports in Nigeria,** iUniverse, Bloomington, Indiana, 2018.

15. **Physics of Soccer II: Science and Strategies for a Better Game**, 2018.

16. **Kitchen Dynamics: The Rice Way**, iUniverse, Bloomington, Indiana, 2015.

17. **Consumer Economics: The Value of Dollars and Sense for Money Management**, iUniverse, Bloomington, Indiana, 2015.

18. **Youth Soccer Training Slides: A Math and Science Approach**, iUniverse, Bloomington, Indiana, 2014.

19. **My Little Blue Book of Project Management**, iUniverse, Bloomington, Indiana, 2014.

20. **8 by 3 Paradigm for Time Management**, iUniverse, Bloomington, Indiana, 2013.

21. **Badiru's Equation of Student Success: Intelligence, Common Sense, and Self-Discipline**, iUniverse, Bloomington, Indiana, 2013.

22. **Isi Cookbook: Collection of Easy Nigerian Recipes**, iUniverse, Bloomington, Indiana, 2013.

23. **Blessings of a Father: Education Contributions of Father Slattery at Saint Finbarr's College**, iUniverse, Bloomington, Indiana, 2013.

24. **Physics in the Nigerian Kitchen: The Science, the Art, and the Recipes**, iUniverse, Bloomington, Indiana, 2013.

25. **The Physics of Soccer: Using Math and Science to Improve Your Game**, iUniverse, Bloomington, Indiana, 2010.
26. **Getting Things Done Through Project Management**, iUniverse, Bloomington, Indiana, 2009.
27. **Blessings of a Father: A Tribute to the Life and Work of Reverend Father Denis J. Slattery**, Heriz Designs and Prints, Lagos, Nigeria, 2005.

Author Biography

Deji Badiru is a Professor Emeritus of Industrial and Systems Engineering. He is a registered Professional Engineer, a certified Project Management Professional, a Fellow of the Institute of Industrial & Systems Engineers, a Fellow of the Industrial Engineering and Operations Management Society, and a Fellow of the Nigerian Academy of Engineering. His academic background consists of BS in Industrial Engineering, MS in Mathematics, and MS in Industrial Engineering and Ph.D. in Industrial Engineering. His areas of interest include mathematical modeling, systems engineering modeling, computer simulation, and productivity analysis. He is a prolific author and a member of several professional associations and scholastic honor societies. Deji holds a US Trademark for DEJI Systems Model for Design, Evaluation, Justification, and Integration.

Dedication

Dedicated to memory of all those who have been lost in traffic wrecks in cities and beyond.

Acknowledgements

I thank and appreciate all the readers who continue to support the titles in the ABICS publications guidebook series. I particularly appreciate and thank Ms. Michaela Finn, who has been my exceptional copyediting assistant for the last four books in the ABICS publications series. She found and corrected many gaffes that I did not realize existed in the raw manuscript. Thank you, Michaela. My equally high gratitude goes to Kaffy Taiwo Rasheed, of Kaffy Studio, Lagos, Nigeria for her original exquisite illustration of a "wreckless" traffic flow that is used on the front cover of this book.

WHAT IS WRECKLESS?

The title "Wreckless in the City" is a humorous play on the words reckless (as in carelessness) and wreck (as in a traffic wreck). The hope is that with the lessons learned in this book, traffic wrecks due to recklessness could be reduced, if not eliminated, on city streets and beyond. Although the guide is primarily for teenage drivers, it is also applicable to all drivers (experienced adults included). Not only will readers learn about safe-driving tips and guidelines, the real science of physics, as it relates to motion, can also be appreciated. If I can get the reader's initial attention through a humorous opening, I will have a chance of retaining the attention through the other critical steps of getting my point across. The goal is to have "wreckless" driving experiences in the city and everywhere else.

Auto accidents are the leading cause of death among teenagers, particularly young men. Worldwide records show that every year, almost two million people are killed in road accidents and about 50 million more are seriously injured.

"Wreckless in the City" is a companion book to the preceding title of "Margin of Death," both in the series of guidebooks from ABICS Publications, self-published by iUniverse. For this book-to-book connectivity, many of the narratives from "Margin of Death" are cannibalized for "Wreckless in the City," for the purpose of re-emphasizing the key points related to the horrible outcomes of road accidents. This is important because young drivers are often under the spell of thinking that they are immortal and taking risks on the road is exciting and of no consequence.

Driving is a privilege and not a right of a status symbol. All drivers must be conscious of the unpleasant possibility of death from road accidents. The intermingling of technical topics and philosophical tenets is by design so that the full scope of driving recklessness could be conveyed. Apart from the driving components of the presentation in this book, teenage drivers, who are often at the high school level of learning science (e.g., physics and mathematics), could benefit from having the additional angles of scientific explanations in this book. Adults and experienced drivers can also benefit from the refresher and/or reconnection presentations of some bygone scientific topics. In this regard, my www.physicsofsoccer.com website has the primary theme of highlighting the transformative power of sports, particularly the widely and wildly loved game of soccer. The concept of wreckless in driving encourages a disciplined approach to driving for teenage drivers . . . and adults too.

The most common post-accident claim is that "the car came out of nowhere." This is a myth. All cars come from somewhere. The fact is that when driving, you should expect the unexpected, and be prepared for other vehicles to come into your space, albeit, uninvited. Non-teenage drivers and other experienced drivers share the road with inexperienced teenage drivers. Therefore, they also need to know useful driving skills and safety tips for sharing the road with teenage drivers. Many times, it takes two to get tangled in a crash. If an experienced driver can help avert and/or mitigate the acts of the other driver, the risk of an actual crash can be reduced.

Many parents that I have shared this concept of "wreckless in the city" with wished they had gotten this cautionary information much earlier to prevent traffic tragedies they had experienced or heard about. Unfortunately, the past cannot be rewritten, but the future can still be guided. Hence, my motivation for writing this book. My goal is for everyone to go "wreckless in the city" everywhere.

Teenagers and Summer Driving

In Summer of 2002, I sent the following letter to the editor of Knoxville New Sentinel in Knoxville, Tennessee.

"Now that another summer has arrived, we need to reopen the discussion of teenagers and summer driving. Because many have written about this issue in the past, I at first thought there was no need to add another enunciation to the same issue. But then, another tragic accident involving teenage drivers occurred recently; and I realized that teenagers have only rudimentary brain functions and it takes several repetitions before instructions can sink in through the cerebral fog.

Teenagers and parents have to realize that ability to control a vehicle does not translate into ability to drive. Driving is not about motor skills required to control a vehicle; but more about cognitive skills for making the right decisions once on the road. Driving comes with many lines of responsibility, a major one of which is the ability to make the right decisions in unrehearsed traffic scenarios. Even though they have licenses certifying that they can control vehicles, most teenagers don't develop driving proficiency until a later age. It is all in the development of reasoning ability that is required to make urgent situational decisions. If this fact is recognized, parents will be more cautious about summer driving freedom of teenagers."

The letter was published, with a retitled caption of "Teenagers aren't good drivers," on July 2, 2006, just before that year's summer driving season. The message of the letter still resonates here today.

Discipline is Essential

With discipline, determination, and focus, drivers can better control outcomes. Some of the most common reasons for traffic accidents include speeding, following too close, and getting distracted. Several years ago, in my academic mentoring of university students, I postulated an equation of success for personal pursuits. The equation simply conveys that success, in anything, is a function of three factors: Natural intelligence, Common sense, and Self-discipline.

$$Success = f(x, y, z)$$

Where f is a functional relationship, x represents natural intelligence (to whatever extent each person is endowed), y represents common sense (which is often based on observatory influences), and z represents self-discipline (which is primarily within the control of the individual, if a concerted effort is made to exercise it). The equation actually works, if it is embraced and practiced. My own personal testimony about self-discipline is conveyed by my case example narrated below.

Teenagers should not drive other teens

I published a newspaper article on the subject of group self-discipline in 2006 in the Knoxville News-Sentinel of

September 8, 2002 with the title of "Teenagers should not drive other teens." The text of that letter goes as follows:

Several fatal accidents involving teenage drivers this summer question the readiness, maturity and peer pressure of teenage drivers. Most of the accidents involved more than one teenager in the vehicle. There is a strong correlation between the number of teenagers in a car and the potential for disaster. When you put two or more teenage minds together, what you get are the acts of a pre-teen child.

Apart from the distraction that a bigger crowd can cause, there is also the propensity to yield to passenger pressure.

A naive comment such as, "You could have made that light," becomes a daring challenge to a teenage driver. Then comes the urge to make the next light, defy the next stop sign, surpass the next speed limit and beat whatever else the road and traffic have to offer. All of these have tragic consequences that a teenage mind cannot fully comprehend. When my grown kids started driving as teenagers, one prerequisite for their driving privilege was having no teenage passengers.

This lone-ranger restriction - as the kids called it - means that the driver is left to focus and concentrate on the task at hand - driving. Unfortunately, with the expanded professional and social responsibilities of two-income families, more and more teenagers embrace the responsibility for their own group transportation.

Consequently, they exhibit greater independence and risk in their driving habits. To avert tragedies, parents must make more efforts to monitor and direct the driving independence of their kids. Don't let them drive in large peer groups.

Common Sense is Required

Haste makes waste and rush makes crash. In almost fifty years of driving on local, rural, back-road, and interstate roadways all over the USA, I have never been involved in any type of accident (knock on wood or knock on paper on the pages of this book); not even fender-benders. I have always practiced defensive-and-avoidant driving habits to avert being involved in accidents. Simple practices such as not following too close, not over-speeding, and being courteous to other drivers can significantly increase the chances of not being involved in a wreck (a la wreckless in the city). It "takes two to tangle," and if one partner is unwilling and uncooperative in the tangling act, road collisions could be minimized. The last time I was pulled over for traffic offense was in 1982 on Interstate 75 somewhere in Georgia, driving seventy-one miles per hour (mph) in a fifty-five-mph speed limit zone. I still believe the stop was unjustified and was instigated by the fact that I was driving my beloved "hot rod," aka 1976 Chevy Camaro Rally Sport. I was pulled over from a long stretch of vehicles moving about the same speed. In other words, I was going with the traffic flow. I vowed since then to never allow myself to be subjected to any other unjustified traffic pullover. I have respected and honored that vow ever since as a show of personal self-discipline. I refer to my conservative driving habits as simply "respecting myself" so that others (especially the traffic police) can respect my space and time.

A couple of hours spent attending to being stopped by a state trooper or sorting out accident details are hours taken away from some other productive pursuits. Over the years, I have been asked how I manage to get so many things done so effortlessly. My usual response is "project management and problem preemption" This simply means using problem preemption techniques to avoid distractions that impede desired undertakings. Problem avoidance makes it possible to devote time to and focus on activities that really matter for achieving goals and objectives.

Playing by the rules up front saves time later to get other things done. Circumventing rules to cut corners can only lead to distractions and the need for time-consuming amendment later on. Time and effort invested in complying with rules and conforming to traffic requirements pays off in the long run. I describe myself as being a "self-imposed compliant conformist." This is a strategy that works by preempting trouble spots that would, otherwise, require a resolution time. There will sometimes be a need for more time-consuming prudence in dotting all i's and crossing all t's upfront before concluding a deal, whatever the "deal" might be. If the prudence is not exercised upfront, it may come back to cause time-consuming resolution attempts and delays later on. Consider accident reconstruction efforts to determine who or what was at fault in a traffic crash.

In the final analysis of getting things done intelligently, the basic approach is to get on with it. There is never a perfect time to get something done. Each opportunity comes with its own constraints. Each constraint may entail its own certain level of necessity. This may be a necessity that must be attended to; such that avoiding the constraints is not possible. If one waits for the perfect time, most things will never get done. We must be willing to compromise, accept trade-offs, and move on. Driving within the posted speed limit is a form of self-discipline to preempt a traffic crash.

The importance of self-discipline and common sense is conveyed by the popular quotes below:

"The three great essentials to achieve anything worthwhile are, first, hard work; second, stick-to-itiveness; third, common sense."
– Thomas A. Edison

"Common sense is in spite of, not the result of, education."
– Victor Hugo

Common sense requires all five senses. To develop and apply common sense when driving, the driver must "feel" his or her environment and have a situational awareness of the prevailing driving condition, as enumerated below:

1. Look to see what is around you.
2. Listen to the sounds of the environment.
3. Touch to appreciate the texture of the surroundings.
4. Smell the scents of the environment. "Smell the roses," so to speak.
5. Taste to appreciate what is available to you.

For one thing, I believe that society is developing an over-reliance on mechanical safety devices, rather than common sense safety practices. Seat belts are just one example. Drivers of cars with four-wheel-drive tend to drive more recklessly in the winter because they believe the extra traction will compensate. Likewise, those who drive SUVs with anti-rollover devices tend to negotiate curves as though they think their devices could overcome the laws of physics.

Rules of Speed Differential

The laws of physics apply to speed on the roadway. A well-informed public is a more intelligent public. In the wake of a deadly car crash that killed six young people in Warren, OH, a driver was interviewed on TV as a part of the community's reaction to the ghastly accident. I was aghast to hear his response that he didn't believe that speed kills (Monday, March 11, 2013, WDTN evening news). He claimed that "speed does not kill; it is speed differential that kills." I beg to differ because his statement is misleading. A quick clarification is needed. I present three simple rules for the ease of public understanding:

1. Yes, speed differential makes a difference.
2. Speed differential makes a bigger difference at higher speeds.
3. Therefore, speed kills.

Without going into the nuances of the laws of motion, consider the speed differential in the collision between a stationary tree (at zero speed) and a car moving at 25 mph. Now, consider the collision of two speeding cars moving at 50 mph and 75 mph, respectively. These are at the same speed differential, but with far different disastrous consequences. There are all kinds of dynamics that come into play in such examples. Actual calculations will reveal that the same speed differential has far more killing potential at higher speeds. So, speed does, indeed, kill. Young drivers should take note.

Intelligence is not Sufficient

Intelligence and skills alone are not sufficient. As the equation of success suggests, all three factors of intelligence, common sense, and discipline must be in effect for a safe-driving outcome to be realized. As necessary and desirable as intelligence is in all our pursuits, it is not sufficient for achieving a "wreckless" in driving. We should not be over-reliant on intelligence.

Obviously, for everyone, the strength of one factor may be higher than the others. Nature has a way of making amendments, such that internal compensations take place to the extent that the overall capability of the individual may still be enhanced. Balancing the senses (factors of success) is essential in safe driving, as I will emphasize throughout this book.

UNPLEASANT HEADLINES

The headlines often read the same or similar, particularly in the early summer months, when teenage drivers typically get their first taste of driving freedom.

"Teen dies in auto wreck."

"Young driver ran off road, hits tree."

"Group of friends involved in accident on curved road."

"Failure to yield leads to wreck."

"Lebanon teen dies after car crashes into tree early on Memorial Day."

"A 17-year-old died after his car hit a light pole late at night."

On and on, the unpleasant headlines continue. Even as I am writing the manuscript for this book while on a train ride from Vienna, Austria to Frankfurt, Germany, on May 16th, 2024, the following paraphrased headline appears in my news feed from my subscription to Dayton Daily News newspaper:

"18-year-old West Carrollton senior killed in Miamisburg crash"

Source citation: Dayton Daily News online news feed, May 16, 2024.

A West Carrollton high school senior riding on a motorcycle died Friday afternoon following a crash near the Dayton Mall in Miamisburg. X (name withheld), 18, was taken to Kettering Health Main Campus, where he was pronounced dead, according to the Ohio State Highway Patrol. Troopers responded around 2:50 p.m. on Friday to the intersection of state route 741/North Springboro Pike and Martins Drive for a crash involving a motorcycle and SUV. A 70-year-old West Carrollton woman driving a 2006 Honda CR-V south on state route 741 when she attempted to turn onto Martins Drive. Rainer was traveling north on state route 741 on a 2021 Yamaha YZF-R3 motorcycle when the two vehicles collided, according to a preliminary investigation by OSHP. Miamisburg police and fire departments assisted troopers at the scene. The crash remains under investigation.

West Carrollton Schools said in a statement, "Our hearts go out to the family of X. He was a West Carrollton Senior due to graduate on May 30th, 2024. His passing will be noted during the graduation ceremony, but final plans have not yet been made. The school district has provided counselors to students and staff during this difficult time.

This reported accident occurred within city limits, not on an expressway out of town, as many of us are often think. Mr. X, unfortunately, did not go "wreckless" in the city. A big sadness. As the title of this book cautions, "and adults too," as adults also cause accidents that can affect young drivers. In the case of X, it is a 70-year-old adult (apparently an experienced driver) who caused the accident. So, adults, just as equally as young drivers, need to learn about the physics of safe driving so that everyone can go "wreckless in the city."

Many parents, grandparents, and extended family members have suffered losses directly or have known someone, who is directly impacted. It is always a devastating reality of mixing driving with inexperience. Even where and when the appropriate driving skills and experience exist, temporary carelessness or inattention could lead to disastrous traffic consequences. While we often highlight the case of inexperienced young drivers, the fact is that many accidents involve adults and experienced drivers.

Adults can get complacent, take things for granted on the roads, and, unexpectedly, be the cause of wrecks. Thus, my message here pertains to both youthful drivers as well as experienced adult drivers.

It is my belief that understanding the "physics" of the road can lead to a better appreciation and respect for potential road dangers and risks. To be fore-warned is to be fore-guarded, so that precautions can be taken.

Considering the concentric circles of impacts, we can see from the inner circle of the immediate family relationships to the extended relationships of family, friends, and colleagues. Thus, the death of one teenage driver impacts a multitude of loved ones.

WHAT ARE THE PHYSICS OF THE ROAD?

Physics, as a science, is defined as the natural science of matter, involving the study of matter, its fundamental constituents, its motion and behavior through space and time, and the related entities of energy and force pertaining to the matter. Physics is one of the most fundamental scientific disciplines, with its main goal being able to understand how things around us behave. In this book, physics refers to how things behave and occur on our road systems. In this case, physics encompasses not only the physical items on the roads, but also the people on the roads. Referring to physics throughout this book will help us recognize the various aspects impinging on what we see and do on the roads. On my physics of soccer website (www.physicsofsoccer.com), I present the following quotes:

"Biology determines what we are, Chemistry
explains what makes us what we are, and
Physics describes what we do."
– Deji Badiru

"Using physics reasoning in soccer gives an edge in
analyzing angles, estimating geometric dimensions,
and anticipating opponents' actions and reactions."
– Deji Badiru

By analogy, the 2008 book, *Factory Physics*, by W.
Hopp and Mark L. Spearman, presents factory physics
as a set of principles that constitute a body of knowledge
on fundamental manufacturing measures, such as cycle
time, throughput, capacity, work-in-process, inventory,
variability, and safety. The authors describe "22 Laws for
Manufacturing" that help managers better understand,
control, and optimize performance of their factories. Thus,
factory physics is a systematic description of the underlying
behavior of manufacturing systems. Understanding it
enables workers to work with the natural tendencies of
manufacturing systems to accomplish the following:

- Identify opportunities for improving existing systems.
- Design effective new systems.
- Make the tradeoffs needed to coordinate policies
  from diverse sources.

In a similar way, this book presents the physics of safe driving in the context of having a better situational awareness of the roads we drive on. This includes the vehicles, the road infrastructure, the traffic system, the signaling processes, the passengers, and the drivers. In effect, the physics of the road requires a systems view of the road.

SYSTEMS VIEW OF THE ROAD

A systems view elicits systems thinking in whatever we do. Systems thinking takes cognizant of the elements contained in the system, whether physical, conceptual, or virtual. So, what is a system?

A system is a collection of interrelated elements, whose collective output (together and in unison) is higher than a mere summation of the individual outputs of the elements. In other words, what we do together on the road, as collaborating road users, is better than what we can accomplish separately and individually. If we maintain a systems mindset on the road, we learn how to coexist on the road, given that some drivers are more careful than others. With systems thinking, we know how to expect the unexpected. We recognize that not all drivers on the road are sane, sober, and alert. We can, thus, adjust our own actions accordingly. We are encouraged to share the road with all the diverse participants on it.

DEJI Systems Model for Safe Driving

At the end of the day, the arena of driving is about systems. Any human engagement consists of systems and subsystems of people, equipment, and process. Using a systems-thinking approach can lead to a better experience and a safe outcome. The DEJI Systems Model is an effective tool to facilitate and drive systems thinking in any organization, enterprise, or pursuit. It is directly applicable to the pursuit of safe driving. The DEJI Systems Model presents a structured strategy for Design, Evaluation, Justification, and Integration. Integration has a special role in achieving and sustaining goals and objectives. The iconic logo of the DEJI Systems Model is presented below.

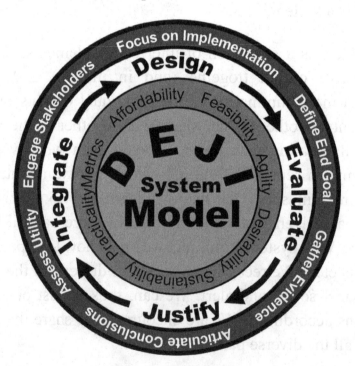

In driving and other endeavors, we must temper idealism with the realities of integration. The next paragraphs present a brief overview of the DEJI Systems Model. Readers can expand each element to enmesh with the specific needs and applications germane to the challenges at hand.

Design

Design in the context of driving is not, necessarily, the typical physical design of an object, but rather the general areas of plans, concepts, ideas, proposals, and so on that represent the desired goals and objectives of the sports operation. In essence, design could represent the concept of a driving habit. Should you or should you not drive?

Evaluation

Evaluation relates an analysis of what constitutes the goals and objectives stated in the design phase. Evaluation is done with respect to the metrics and rubrics appropriate for the specific problem area, for example, driving on a dangerous road. Evaluation may consist of quantitative, qualitative, and/or social factors. For example, the pursuit of equity and justice in driving may necessitate an evaluation along the lines of traffic volume on a particular road system.

Justification

A design (e.g., idea) that appears good in concept and acceptable in evaluation may not be justified for implementation. In this stage of the DEJI Systems Model, such things as desirability, acceptability, repeatability, affordability, sustainability, and sociability may come into play in the justification of a proposed driving plan.

Integration

Integration is the final stage of the DEJI Systems Model, where we consider if and how everything fits together. A plan that is implemented out of phase or in disconnection with the prevailing operating environment cannot stand the test of time and safety. The structured process of the DEJI Systems Model can help to identify the points of disconnection earlier on so that remedies can be explored, or alternate plans (and modifications) developed.

Ideas (designs, concepts, proposals, etc.) that are good in principle often don't integrate well into the realities of a sustainable implementation. Therein lies the case for systems integration as advocated by the DEJI Systems Model. As an author, my love of systems integration is predicated on the belief that you can fight to get what you want and get hurt in the fighting process, or you can systematically negotiate and win without shedding tears, blood, or sweat. It is in systems integration that we get things done to assure safety on the roads and elsewhere. In a systems context, integration is everything. Several practical examples exist to ginger our interest in systems integration. One common (and relatable) example is in the behavior of drivers. Integration implies monitoring, adapting to, and reacting to the prevailing scenario in interstate road traffic. In this case, integration calls for observing and enmeshing into the ongoing traffic with respect to flow and speed. If everyone drives with a sense of traffic systems integration, there will be fewer accidents on the road. In the full DEJI systems framework, a driver would observe and design (i.e., formulate) driving actions, evaluate the rationale and potential consequences of the "designed" actions, justify (mentally) why the said actions are necessary and pertinent for the current traffic scenario, and then integrate the actions to the driving condition.

Integration is the basis for the success of any system. This is particularly critical for system of systems (SoS) applications where there may be many moving parts. A familiar example is the January 2022 announcement of the retirement of USA Supreme Court Justice Stephen Breyer. Justice Breyer was known as a legal pragmatist, who worked to make the law work in consonance with how society lives and works. That is a good spirit of aligning and integrating the law with people's lives and expectations. When a system is aligned with reality, the probability of success increases exponentially. When driving actions and habits are integrated with the prevailing traffic conditions, better and safer driving results can be achieved.

The premise of systems thinking is that integration across a system is the overriding requirement for a successful system of systems (SoS). A system is represented as consisting of multiple parts, all working together for a common purpose or goal. Systems can be small or large, simple, or complex. Small devices can also be considered systems. Systems have inputs, processes, and outputs. Systems are usually explained using a model for visual clarification inputs, process, and outputs. A systems model helps illustrate the major elements and their relationships.

Systems engineering is the application of engineering tools and techniques to the solutions of multi-faceted problems through a systematic collection and integration of parts of the problem with respect to the lifecycle of the problem. It is the branch of engineering concerned with the development, implementation, and use of large or complex data sets across diverse domains. It focuses on specific goals of a system considering the specifications, prevailing constraints, expected services, possible behaviors, and structure of the system. It also involves a consideration of the activities required to ensure that the system's performance matches specified goals. Systems engineering addresses the integration of tools, people, and processes required to achieve a cost-effective and timely operation of the system.

Some of the features of systems thinking include solution to multi-faceted problems, a holistic view of a problem domain, applications to both small and large problems, decomposition of complex problems into smaller manageable chunks, direct considerations for the pertinent constraints that exist in the problem domain, systematic linking of inputs to goals and outputs, explicit treatment of the integration of tools, people, and processes, and a compilation of existing systems engineering models. A typical decision support model is a representation of a system, which can be used to answer questions about the system. The end result of using a systems engineering approach in driving is to integrate a solution into the normal organizational process. In a nutshell, the following questions highlight the importance of using a systems-thinking approach in driving, where the diversity of people, equipment, and process is prevalent.

- What level of trade-offs on the level of integration are tolerable?
- What is the incremental cost of pursuing higher integration?
- What is the marginal value of higher integration?
- What is the adverse impact of a failed integration attempt?
- What is the value of integration of system characteristics over time?

In the context of driving, presented below are guidelines and important questions relevant for road safety systems integration.

- What are the unique characteristics of each component in the integrated system?
- How do the characteristics complement one another?
- What physical interfaces exist among the components?
- What data and information interfaces exist among the components?
- What ideological differences exist among the components?
- What are the data flow requirements for the components?
- What internal and external factors are expected to influence the integrated system?
- What are the relative priorities assigned to each component of the integrated system?
- What are the strengths and weaknesses of the integrated system?
- What resources are needed to keep the integrated system operating satisfactorily?
- Which organizational unit has primary responsibility for the integrated system?

In summary, asking questions before jumping into any aspect of driving is essential for realizing desired goals and objectives. May the constructive force of the road be with all drivers positively.

DRINKING AND DRIVING DON'T MIX

Some drunk drivers have unceremoniously and erroneously quoted Benjamin Franklin in the silly humor of their acts.

"BEER is proof the God loves us and
wants us to be HAPPY."

No record exists about Benjamin Franklin saying this quote. In his time, he had better things to worry about. The quote is a fabrication that first appeared on the internet in the late 1990s. Despite being attributed to Franklin on tee-shirts and other restaurant merchandise, there is no reliable source attributing the quote to him. Benjamin Franklin was an American polymath, a leading writer, scientist, inventor, statesman, diplomat, printer, publisher, and political philosopher. Among the most influential intellectuals of his time, Franklin was one of the Founding Fathers of the United States, and a drafter and signer of the Declaration of Independence. He was also the first postmaster general of the United States.

Benjamin Franklin's focus was on doing a lot of good things for a lot of people and places. I urge readers to dismiss the quote as a celebratory model of behavior. It is not within the morale advocated by the theme of this book. The quote does not fit the physics of safe driving promoted here. The fact is that drinking (of any kind) and driving don't mix. Just don't do it. The consequences are grievous, even for experienced and skilled drivers. Thousands of precious lives are lost every year worldwide due to drunken-related road accidents, despite the enforcement actions of government authorities. It is hoped that presenting the message in terms of the "physics of safe driving" may make drivers pay more attention to the rights and wrongs of driving, from a physical science perspective. Presenting the same message in a variety of ways on diverse platforms may help to get the message across, such as my quotes below:

"The sturdier the glass, the more shatter
it makes when it breaks."
– Deji Badiru

"Haste makes waste, just as rush makes ruins in a crash."
– Adedeji Badiru

If you think you have the skills and ability to manage your drinking, recognize the consequences that could be out of your control. According to the physical consequences of a road wreck, no one has the hulk to handle a crash. Drinking and driving don't mix. Just don't do it. You can drink responsibly at home and at controlled social events, just don't get on the road when you are over the edge of alcohol consumption.

People who would never think of killing themselves or killing someone else sometimes get behind the wheel and do just that. They run the risk of killing themselves and others.

THE PHYSICS OF MOTION

The most celebrated lessons about the physics of motion are conveyed by Newton's Laws of Motion, which Sir Isaac Newton first postulated in 1687 in this book, *Mathematical Principles of Natural Philosophy*. Newton used the laws to investigate and explain the motion of many physical objects and systems. I have used the laws extensively on my Physics of Soccer website (www.physicsofsoccer.com), which highlights the transformative power of sports in education. Sir Isaac Newton, who lived from 1642 to 1726, was an English polymath.

Newton was a mathematician, physicist, astronomer, alchemist, theologian, and author. He was described as a natural philosopher. He was an influential person in the scientific revolution and social enlightenment of his time. His pioneering book, *Mathematical Principles of Natural Philosophy* (1687), consolidated many previous results and established classical mechanics. Newton also made seminal contributions to optics, and shares credit with German mathematician Gottfried Wilhelm Leibniz for developing infinitesimal calculus, though he developed calculus years before Leibniz. Newton used his mathematical description of gravity to derive Kepler's laws of planetary motion, account for tides, the trajectories of comets, the precession of the equinoxes and other phenomena. He demonstrated that the motion of objects on Earth and celestial bodies could be accounted for by the same principles. Newton's three famous laws of motion are summarized below:

Newton's First law

An object at rest tends to stay at rest and an object in motion tends to stay in motion with the same speed and in the same direction unless acted upon by an unbalanced force.

Newton's Second law

The acceleration of an object as produced by a net force is directly proportional to the magnitude of the net force, in the same direction as the net force, and inversely proportional to the mass of the object. Force is equal to mass times acceleration.

Newton's Third law

For every action, there is an equal and opposite reaction.

The science and physics behind playing soccer more intellectually is the same that can be applied to many ball-based sports, such as baseball, cricket, basketball, badminton, handball, table tennis, tennis, golf, volleyball, and football. While each sport has its own unique characteristics, the same principles of science govern movements of the ball. Some interesting physics principles are summarized below as suggested further reading:

Motion and range of the ball are controlled by force and acceleration principles in accordance with Newton's Laws of Motion.

The spin on the ball in bat-and-ball collision is a function of the impact force as well as the angle of the point of impact.

Surface smoothness of the ball, gravity, wind speed, and wind direction directly influence level of air resistance and the behavior of the ball in flight.

In a baseball pitch, the flight path of the ball is a function of spin, out-curve, and in-curve placed on the ball by the pitcher.

There are physics-based curvature properties on fastball, curveball, slider, and screwball.

For a given velocity of impact on the ball, the shape compression on the ball is proportional to the change in velocity of the ball. The basic elements of STEM are:

- Science
- Technology
- Engineering
- Mathematics

How do all these affect sports? Coupling the learning experience of STEM with the fun of sports participation makes the overall process much more effective and rewarding in both directions.

Science.

Science (from the Latin scientia, meaning "knowledge") refers to any systematic knowledge or practice. In its more usual interpretation, science refers to a system of acquiring knowledge based on scientific methods, as well as the organized body of knowledge gained through such research. Science consists of two major categories:

- Experimental science.
- Applied science.

Experimental science is based on experiments (Latin: experiri, "to try out") as a method of investigating causal relationships among variables and factors. Applied science is the application of scientific research to specific human needs. Experimental science and applied science are often interconnected.

Science is the effort to discover and increase human understanding of how the real-world works. Its focus is on reality which is independent of religious, political, cultural, or philosophical preferences. Using controlled methods, scientists collect data in the form of observations, record observable physical evidence of natural phenomena, and analyze the information to construct theoretical explanations of how things work. Knowledge in science is gained through research. The methods of scientific research include the generation of conjectures (hypotheses) about how something works. Experimentations are conducted to test these hypotheses under controlled conditions. The outcome of this empirical scientific process is the formulation of theory that describes human understanding of physical processes and facilitates prediction of what to expect in certain situations. A broader and more modern definition of science includes the natural sciences along with the social and behavioral sciences, as the main subdivisions. This involves the observation, identification, description, experimental investigation, and theoretical explanation of a phenomenon. The social and behavioral aspects of team-based soccer make it particularly amenable to the application of science in its broad sense. The five steps of the scientific method are provided below:

1. Ask a question or identify a problem. A scientist can learn about a sports scenario by observing.
2. Gather underlying data and conduct background research related to the problem identified. This is useful for designing the pertinent experiments.
3. Form a hypothesis, as an educated guess, to answer the question posed in Step 1.
4. Conduct the experiment and record the observations to test the hypothesis, in which case there is one variable that is set as the factor of interest (dependent variable), while the other factors are held constant, as a control.
5. Draw a conclusion to state if the hypothesis is true or false.

For example, if a sports recruiter presents a prospective player and proclaims him (or her) to be fit for a team, a hypothesis can be developed and tested (via a practice drill) to determine if the hypothesis is true or false.

Physics, one of the most-recognized branches of science, is derived from the Greek word, physis (meaning "nature") is the natural science which explains fundamental concepts of mass, charge, matter, and its motion; as well as and all properties that arise from the concepts, such as energy, force, space, and time. Physics is the general analysis of nature, conducted to understand how the physical world behaves. Physics is a major player (pun intended) in STEM, and it deserves special treatment and understanding. Principles of Physics are embedded in or complemented by several other scientific bodies of knowledge such as astronomy, chemistry, mathematics, and biology. This symbiotic relationship causes the boundaries of physics to remain difficult to distinguish. Physics is significant and influential because it provides an understanding of things that we see, observe, and use every day such as television, computers, cars, household appliances, and sports. The game of soccer is subject to many of the principles of Physics.

Physics covers a wide range of phenomena of nature, from the smallest (e.g., sub-atomic particles) to the largest (e.g., galaxies). Included in this are the very basic objects from which all other things develop. It is because of this that physics is sometimes said to be the "fundamental science". Physics helps to describe the various phenomena that occur in nature in terms of easier-to-understand phenomena. Thus, physics aims to link the things we see around us to their origins or root causes. It then tries to link the root causes together to find an ultimate reason for why nature is the way it is. It is to the end that I offer the quotes below:

"Biology determines what we are, Chemistry explains what makes us what we are, and Physics describes what we do." - Deji Badiru, Soccer Author

"Using physics reasoning in soccer gives an edge in analyzing angles, estimating geometric dimensions, and anticipating opponents' actions and reactions." - Deji Badiru, Soccer Author

The ancient Chinese observed that certain rocks (i.e., lodestone) were attracted to one another by some invisible force. This effect was later called magnetism and was first rigorously studied in the 17th century. A little earlier than the Chinese, the ancient Greeks knew of other objects such as amber, that when rubbed with fur would cause a similar invisible attraction between the two. This was also first studied rigorously in the 17th century and came to be called electricity. Thus, physics had come to understand two observations of nature in terms of some root cause (electricity and magnetism). However, further work in the 19th century revealed that these two forces were just two different aspects of one force – electromagnetism. This process of unifying or linking forces of nature continues today in contemporary studies of Physics.

Technology

A strict definition of technology is quite elusive. In its basic form, it relates to how humans develop and use tools. Knowledge and usage of tools and crafts constitute the application of knowledge. Technology is a term with origins in the Greek word "technologia," formed from *techne*, ("craft") and *logia*, ("saying"). Technology can refer to material objects of use by society, such as machines, hardware, or utensils. It can also encompass broad areas covering systems, methods of organization, and techniques. The term can be applied generally or to specific areas of application, including:

- Communication technology (e.g., wireless phones)
- Construction technology (e.g., road systems)
- Medical technology (e.g., x-ray imaging)
- Weapons technology (e.g., firearm)

The origin of the use of technology by humans dates to the conversion of natural resources into simple tools (e.g., stones to arrow heads). The pre-historical discovery of the ability to control fire increased the available sources of food. The invention of the wheel helped humans to travel long distances from their home base. The development of roofs enabled humans to control their environment and construct living quarters. Technological advances have minimized physical barriers to communication and allowed humans to interact quicker and more effectively. The capability of technology often advances on a geometric scale. Technology has facilitated more advanced economies that benefit the entire society, such as the emerging global economy. Technology has made it possible for us to have more leisure time and better working conditions.

Engineering

Engineering is the body of knowledge related to the science of making, using, and improving things. It is the discipline and profession of applying technical, scientific, and mathematical knowledge to utilize natural laws and physical resources to help design and implement materials, structures, machines, devices, systems, and processes that safely realize a desired objective. Engineers not only build these things, but they also embark upon improving them. For example, industrial engineers pride themselves on the following quote:

> "Engineers make things, industrial
> engineers make things better."

Engineering dates back thousands of years and it is created as the origin of modern human development as it exists today. Engineering has been practiced since prehistoric times. The basic steps in the engineering problem-solving methodology consist of the following:

Step 1: Gather data and information pertinent to the problem.
Step 2: Develop an explicit Problem Statement.
Step 3: Identify what is known and unknown.
Step 4: Specify assumptions and circumstances.
Step 5: Develop schematic representations and drawings of inputs and outputs.

Step 6: Perform engineering analysis using equations and models as applicable.

Step 7: Compose a cogent articulation of the results.

Step 8: Perform verification, presentation, and "selling" of the result.

These steps are very much in alignment with what is needed in managing sports enterprises of any sort everywhere. The steps may be tweaked, condensed, or expanded depending on the specific problem being tackled. The good thing about the engineering process is that technical, social, political, economic, and managerial considerations can be factored into the process. The end justifies the details at hand. Based on our recommended approach of approaching problems from a systems perspective, we add the following capstone requirement to the engineering problem-solving steps:

Capstone Step: Integrate the solution into the normal operating landscape of the organization. It is through systems integration that a sustainable actualization of the result can be achieved as a contribution to national development.

Engineering has a lot to offer, particularly in the context of connecting the dots in the technical, administrative, economic, and social aspects of a problem. The simple mathematical expression below conveys the engineering framework:

$$f(x, y, z, \ldots) = output$$

The variables in the equation are explained as follows:

f is mathematical function of several variables

$x, y, z, \ldots$, etc. are the pertinent variables related to the problem of interest.

output is the expected result of the mathematical function operating on the pertinent variables.

An implementation of any initiative without connecting the applicable dots is doomed to fail. The common characteristics of engineers through the centuries have been an interest in exploratory engagements and intellectual curiosity about how to build things, both physical and conceptual. Common engineering inquiries include:

- What?
- Who?
- Where?
- Why?
- When?
- How?

These inquiries are sometimes represented by the following mnemonic W^5H (w five h). Due to its wide applications, engineering is very diverse and ubiquitous in human endeavors. The major branches of engineering offer a variety of career fields and options, including the following:

- Aerospace engineering
- Agricultural engineering
- Architectural engineering
- Astronautical engineering
- Bio-medical engineering
- Ceramic engineering
- Chemical engineering
- Civil engineering
- Electrical engineering
- Geological engineering
- Industrial engineering
- Marine engineering
- Materials engineering
- Mechanical engineering
- Metallurgical engineering
- Mining engineering
- Nuclear engineering
- Petroleum engineering
- Systems Engineering

Mathematics

Mathematics is the foundation for applying science, technology, and engineering to solve problems. It is the study of quantity, structure, space, change, and related topics of pattern and form. Mathematicians seek out patterns, whether found in numbers, space, natural science, computers, imaginary abstractions, or elsewhere.

Mathematicians formulate new conjectures and establish their truth by precise deduction from axioms and definitions that are chosen based on the prevailing problem scenario. The most common branches of mathematics for everyday applications are:

- Algebra
- Calculus
- Geometry
- Trigonometry
- Differential equations

Algebra is the mathematics of quantities (known and unknown). Calculus is the mathematics of variations (i.e., changes in variables). Geometry is the mathematics of size, shape, and relative position of figures and with properties of space. Trigonometry is the mathematics of triangles and their angles (interior and exterior). It is the study of how the sides and angles of a triangle interrelate to one another. A differential equation is a mathematical equation for an unknown function of one or several variables that relates the values of the function itself and its derivatives of various orders. Differential equations play a prominent role in engineering, physics, economics, and other disciplines. A practical example of the application of differential equations is the modeling of the acceleration of a soccer ball falling through the air (considering only gravity and air resistance). Everything up must come down, . . . eventually, so the saying goes; but there is science behind the saying.

General Physics of Objects in Motion

A good analogy for how the laws of motion affect the movement and interaction of objects can be found in ball-based sports, such as soccer, basketball, and tennis. Movements and interactions of larger objects, such as cars involved in a wreck, follow the same basic laws.

For example, a spinning ball performing a three-dimensional spatial motion typically experiences at least four forces, namely an aerodynamic drag, a buoyant force, a gravitational force, and the Magnus force. The Magnus force was first studied by Robins Magnus. This force acts perpendicular to the direction of the ball's velocity vector and causes the deflection of the spinning spheroidal ball object as a result of which, the ball experiences a whirlpool of rotating air about its spin axis. This circulating air slows down the ball motion and the air flow.

Multi-physics studies provide insights into the theory of projectile motion for the inflight spheroidal ball. The ball in motion experiences four forces expressible based on Newton's second law with the net force in a vector form. I will not provide all the gory details of the mathematical representations of motion in this book. It suffices just to know that strange and interesting things can happen when two objects, such as two speeding vehicles, collide. Sparks fly. Energy gets transferred. Heat is generated. Objects get distorted. Lives can get ruined. While in many textbooks of physics or calculus, the analysis of the trajectories of objects is commonly addressed by assuming the absence of air resistance, it is invariably the case, however, that drag forces affect the path of a spheroidal ball and are of two main types: skin friction drag, and pressure drag. Skin friction occurs when adherence of air molecules to the surface of the ball occurs, resulting in friction from the interaction of the two bodies. The resistance resulting from pressure drag occurs due to the separation of air streams around the moving object resulting in different velocities in the air streams above and below the object, which recombine at the rear of the object in motion. These two elements of drag forces affect horizontal distance of travel and the Reynolds number for the spheroidal ball travel. If the above narrative whets the intellectual appetite of the reader, I recommend further reading on the subject matter of the physics of motion.

ORGANIZING, THE JAPANESE WAY

If we are well organized, we can be safer, not only at work, but also at home and on the roads. Safe driving is as much a process of managing a project (at the personal level) as managing complex projects at the corporate level. Each instance of project management requires a discipline of purpose, which requires a high level of self-organization. If you are well organized, the pressure to rush and drive recklessly is mitigated. In this section, I enlist the Japanese principle of "5s" to emphasize the connection between safe and meticulous driving and the commitment to being organized upfront. Discipline is within the driver's control, but it requires dedication, commitment, a positive attitude, seriousness, and perseverance. Success comes from self-discipline. Self-discipline is a cornerstone of sustainable success. Discipline is what helps you to get up in the morning and set out to do the day's chores . . . even when you'd rather continue sleeping. Discipline is what gets you started with your task at the appropriate early time so that a rushed pursuit does not ensue. Discipline is what helps you overcome uninvited temptation to speed recklessly when the road ahead of you is open and free. Even if you are driving on the speed-unlimited German Autobahn (express highway), you still need self-discipline to caution yourself to drive at a safe speed. In May 2024, a friend took my wife and me for driving spin on the German Autobahn from Frankfurt to Koblenz. It was a scary experience, despite the assurance of safety. The outer express lane of the Autobahn allows drivers to go as fast as they care to go. The safety assurance comes with the fact that all cars driving in that lane are equally super-speedy-fast. The rationale is that if the flow is maintained by all drivers in the fast lane, the chance of an erratic accident is minimized. I am not convinced because there is still a high rate of accidents on the German Autobahn. One recent headline reads, "Car crash with 240km/hr (149 miles/hour) on German Autobahn)."

Yes, refusing temptation is within the driver's control.

Discipline helps people avoid excess drinking, eating, spending, and other undesirable indulgences.

Be mindful that "five minutes of temporary pleasure can lead to an everlasting sorrow of a loss." Don't put the fun before the pain.

The single most important requirement for getting things done is self-commitment. It is through the discipline of self-commitment that projects, both large and small (e.g., driving), can be executed successfully. Without self-commitment nothing can be accomplished satisfactorily and safely. A rush can make a haste and a waste.

As a case in point, the number of those receiving project management training and certification is increasing rapidly. However, the number of project failures, with significant cost, schedule, and performance implications, is also increasing. This is a fact that is inconsistent with the theory and conventional expectations. If there is no self-commitment to execute a project according to plan, no amount of education, training, credentialing, tools, and techniques can rescue the goals and objectives. Those who are most eloquent about what needs to be done, and how, are often the ones who falter when it comes to actually doing it. Each person must dedicate themselves and commit to completing tasks and projects correctly, possibly ahead of time and safely.

Nothing demonstrates self-discipline more than being organized. There are many guides for getting organized. In the corporate environment, there are formal tools and techniques of pursuing a disciplined approach to work. In this section, I leverage the rigorous Japanese technique of "5s/6s." The belief is that these tools, applied on the small scale of personal needs, such as driving safely, would be just as effective as they have been in the corporate work environment.

The "5s" and "6s" methodologies are Japanese techniques that demonstrate workplace discipline through a series of words starting with the letter "s." When the first five words are used, we have "5s" and when six words are used, we have "6s." The connection of this to safe driving habits is that being organized facilitates the commitment to safe and unrushed actions. The elements of "5s" are explained below:

1. **Seiri (Sort):** This means to distinguish between what is needed and not needed and remove the latter. The tools and materials in the workplace are sorted out. The unwanted tools and materials are placed in the tag area.

2. **Seiton (Stabilize):** This means to enforce a place for everything. The workplace is organized by labeling. The machines and tools are labeled with their names and all the sufficient data required. A sketch with exact scale of the work floor is drawn with grids. This helps in achieving a better flow of work and easy access of all tools and machines.

3. **Seison (Shine):** This means to clean up the workplace and look for ways to keep it clean. Periodic cleaning and maintenance of the workplace and machines are done. The wastes are placed in a separate area. The recyclable and other wastes are placed in separate containers. This makes it easy to remember where all components are

placed. The clean look of the workplace helps with better organization and increases flow.

4. **Seiketsu (Standardize):** This means to maintain and monitor adherence to the first three "s's." This process helps standardize work. The work of each person is clearly defined. The suitable person is chosen for a particular job. People in the workplace should know who is responsible for what. The scheduling is standardized. Time is maintained for every job that is to be completed. A set of rules is created to maintain the first "3s's." This helps in improving efficiency of the workplace.

5. **Shitsuke (Sustain):** This means follow the rules to keep the workplace 6s-right—"maintain the gain." Once the previous "4s" are implemented some rules are developed for sustaining the other "S's."

6. **Safety:** This refers to eliminating hazards in the work environment. The sixth "s" is added so that focus could be directed at safety within all improvement efforts. This is particularly essential in high-risk and accident-prone environments. This sixth extension is often debated as a separate entity because safety should be implicit in everything we do. Besides, the Japanese word for Safety is "Anzen," which does not follow the "s" rhythm. Some practitioners even include additional "s's". So, we could have "8s" with the addition of Security and Satisfaction.

7. **Security**: e.g., job security, personal security, mitigation of risk, capital security, intellectual security, property security, information security, asset security, equity security, product brand security, etc.

8. **Satisfaction**: e.g., employee satisfaction, morale, job satisfaction, sense of belonging, etc.

How to Apply Self-Discipline.

- Think of the possible consequence of your actions.
- Don't allow friends, leisure, and recreation "occupy" too much of your study time.

Badiru's Four Read-Through Guide: This is my discipline-based guide for taking a test. It centers on reading a test question thoroughly before attempting to solve the test problem. Read a test question again and again before attempting to answer the question. The four-read-through guide suggests reading a test question four times and it goes as follows:

- Read the test question for the first time, just for general orientation to the question.
- Read the question the second time, to note and/or jot down the essential points or data.
- Read the question the third time. At this point, you should attempt to solve the problem By this time, you would have seen the question "twice" before. This

allows for a better understanding of the problem and all the requirements, givens, and unknowns.

- Read the question the fourth time. During this stage, do a recapitulation of the problem, the boundary conditions, and a confirmation that you have answered the question as instructed.

One common example of the pitfall of not reading a question in its entirety is the famous twenty-question test, in which the first instruction says to read every question before attempting to answer any of them. The last instruction says you don't have to answer any of the questions. Most students will impatiently start answering the questions as fast as they can, because of the time constraint specified for the test. In the end, students never reach the end of the 20 questions within the time allotted for the test when, in fact, the test consists of only reading the 20 questions without having to do anything. Valuable time and stress are expended trying to beat the test time. This represents a misapplication of effort and time. It takes a great amount of self-discipline to completely read a question before attempting to solve it. If the time is invested, it can save a lot of agony later.

It is all about self-discipline.

Discipline of time management is essential for educational success.

Time is the basis for everything. It cannot be regained. My poem below presents the importance of time management.

The Flight of Time

What is the speed and direction of Time?

Time flies; but it has no wings.

Time goes fast; but it has no speed.

Where has time gone? But it has no destination.

Time goes here and there; but it has no direction.

Time has no embodiment. It neither flies, walks, nor goes anywhere.

Yet, the passage of time is constant."

    – © 2006 by Adedeji Badiru

Time is of the essence when managing your academic tasks. Task management can be viewed as a three-legged stool with the following main components:

- Time availability
- Resource allocation
- Quality of performance

When one leg is shorter than the others or non-existent, the stool cannot be used for its expected purpose. Time is a limited non-recyclable commodity, as evidenced by the opening poem. Industry leaders send employees to time management training sessions and continuously preach the importance of completing tasks on time. However, one area. where time management is most crucial, that is often overlooked and undervalued, is personal task management. Task management, by definition, is in itself time management via milestone tracking of important accomplishments and bottleneck identification. There are only twenty-four hours in a day and one of the goals for a student is how to use those twenty-four hours efficiently. The tendency is for students to sacrifice time in their academic pursuits and still expect the same level of performance. This thought process is flawed and ultimately leads to failure. If an academic semester task that normally takes 12 weeks for completion is condensed into 4 weeks, this would represent a time compression of more than 60 percent. If we were to take the task management stool and reduce one of the legs by 60 percent, the stool would topple over. This is the same result, in terms of performance, when activity compression occurs. An analysis of time constraints should be a part of the student's feasibility assessment of his or her study responsibilities. Task planning, personal organization, and task scheduling all have a timing component. If the timing component of a project is missed, a tendency to rush and expedite activities may result. Thereby creating the potential for a rush, which can lead to a wreck. Understanding and managing the precedence relationships among activities can help us in managing and controlling our activities and getting them onto a smooth path. Thereby mitigating the need to rush, speed, and risk a crash. In essence, doing a better job of project management can defuse rushing and speeding on the roadways.

The precedence relationships among tasks fall into three major categories which include technical precedence, procedural precedence, and imposed precedence. Technical precedence requirements reflect the technical relationships among activities. For example, in conventional construction, walls must be erected before the roof can be installed. Procedural precedence requirements, however, are determined by policies and procedures that may be arbitrary or subjective and may have no concrete justification. Imposed precedence requirements can be classified as resource-imposed, project status-imposed, or environment-imposed. For example, resource shortages may require that one task be completed before another can begin, or the status of a project (e.g., percent completion) may determine that one activity be performed before another. The physical environment of a project, such as weather changes or the effects of concurrent projects, may determine the precedence relationships of the activities in the project. An assessment of how tasks interrelate is a required element of not wasting time in task scheduling and management in the pursuit of sustainable education.

FROM THE MARGIN OF DEATH

As mentioned in the introduction of this book, sections from a preceding guidebook, *Margin of Death*, are repeated here for relevance and currency of topics. To whatever extent the gory details of death are presented, re-presented, and repeated, the more likely the message of caution should be imbibed from different platforms.

Margin of Death is a cautionary note on death being a slim margin away in the activities we engage in, particularly driving. The book presents safety and life preservation tips to avoid, minimize, or mitigate accidental disasters that could rob people of their precious lives. Although the topic is serious and unnerving, this book is written in a humorous tone, perhaps to put readers at ease. Life is always at risk from a variety of sources, ranging from accidental, negligent, and deliberate acts. While natural age-driven death is accepted, we should minimize exposure to other non-scheduled, life-robbing incidents, a majority of which are manmade. On the natural expectation of death, Nepal's Dalai Lama says the following:

> *"Worrying about death is a waste of*
> *time. Death is a part of life."*
> – Dalai Lama

A near miss is the one we are aware of, but the narrow margins are the ones we never know.

Life is a transient asset: it comes and goes. It can be gone in a flash, when least expected, and particularly when tragic events happen, such as road accidents. This written piece is motivated by a near-miss road experience that could have led to a disastrous outcome. As a prolific author, I had, for many years, harbored the idea of writing an advisory book on the "margin of death" to caution readers about the frailty of life, based on multiple incidents seen, observed, and reported in society. We tend to take life for granted, which we need to rethink. Writing about the "margin of death" helps us recognize and appreciate how fleeting and short life can be. The tranquility and serenity of life can be snuffed out in an instant.

This is a story of how close to death humans come each day, sometimes without knowing it. It provides facts and fiction of the narrow escapes, close calls, and near-miss events that people never know about. You could turn the corner and escape just in the nick of time, when death (by whatever means) is lurking nearby.

For example, you are being targeted by robbers at a deserted train station in a bad neighborhood. You stand there, with no worries in the world, waiting for the midnight train. The train arrives, the door opens, you get in, and the door closes. The robbers are hurrying to catch up with you, but they are locked out of the train. You go on with your journey, unaware of the fate that nearly befell you.

Although many dangers to life exist in all facets of human existence, the opening case example in this book is about the dangers of the roads of transportation around the world. Road accidents create havoc all over the world. So much so that several YouTube channels present programs on "the most dangerous roads in the world." Such programs are tragically exhilarating, and provide cautionary notes about road travels and accidents. Unpleasantly, a majority of the most dangerous roads are located in developing and underdeveloped parts of the world. When roads in developed nations fall into the category of most dangerous, it is often due to road congestion, weather-related mishaps, and driver errors rather than the physical infrastructure of the roads. As more efforts are directed toward making roads safer, we see more and more impaired drivers on the roads. The quote below conveys that the more efforts that are made on road infrastructures, the more danger may lurk on the roads due to the flaws of humans, who tend to take things for granted.

> "The sturdier the glass, the more shatter
> it makes when it breaks."
> – Deji Badiru

The sensitivity highlighted in this book could help us all be more conscious of our driving habits, environments, and our individual and collective responsibilities on the roads. Each road danger presents a narrow margin of death. Therein lies the theme conveyed in the title of this book.

For example, the widely-publicized hydroelectric dam collapses in Brazil, Kenya, Cameroon, and other places have caused loss of lives, in unanticipated ways. These unfortunate incidents represent margins of death that people could be exposed to in dam areas.

Other quotes of relevance are shared below:

> "The reality of life is death."
> – Deji Badiru

> "The reality of death is just a stone throw
> away within a narrow margin."
> – Deji Badiru

> "Avoid hurried worries in harried times."
> – Deji Badiru

Story telling is often an effective way to get points and guidelines across. For this reason, my writing style in this book follows my usual story telling pattern, which is popularly admired by friends and colleagues as "Deji-Vu" stories. "Deji-Vu" is a fun play on the popular social buzz of "Déjà-Vu," a French phrase that describes a familiarity with situations one hasn't experienced before. Some people even carry the Deji style to the full buzz of "Deji vu, all over again." Yes, even if I have told the same story before, it helps the mental retention of my audience to hear it again. Thus, I am proud of the effectiveness of "Deji vu, all over again."

The initial story of focus in this book is a near-miss incident that my wife and I experienced in January 2024 in Lagos, Nigeria. I have had it in mind to write on the "margin of death" for many years, but I never got around to it due to conflicting priorities. The last straw that finally sparked my inspiration for writing this book is the incident narrated in the following paragraphs.

It was a pleasant and clear afternoon on a major road leading to the important bridge connecting the mainland and the Island of Lagos, Nigeria. Traffic was flowing smoothly with a diverse combination of all types of vehicles. My wife and I were in the back seats of a Jeep, driven by an experienced and attentive driver, for whom we had the affectionate nickname of "Baba Olokere." The driver's old-fashioned mobile phone invited such a humorous nickname. His phone was of a caliber below the old flip phones and he adoringly referred to his phone as "Okere," which meant "Squirrel" in functionality comparison to modern smartphones. For this, we jokingly called him "Baba Olokere," which means owner of a squirrel. He couldn't do much with the phone, but it worked for him and his most basic needs of making and receiving phone calls. Safety on the roads requires a driver's rapt attention. This focused attention probably saved our lives on this particular day.

This short road trip was initiated by a dinner invitation from a family friend living on the Lagos Island portion of Lagos, a crowded city of over twenty-three million inhabitants, according to the 2024 estimate by worldpopulationreview. com. Sixteen million are estimated to reside in Lagos proper with another nine million residing in the general urban area. It is a mega city with chaotic and jumbled transportation infrastructures. To make it through each disorderly road on any day is to toy with the narrow margin of death. To be fair, the same could be said about many other mega cities around the world, including Cairo, Egypt, Karashi, Pakistan, and Chicago, Illinois, U.S.A. Traffic congestion can make any city dangerous for travelers. The higher the population density, the more horrendous the traffic profile, which, consequently, leads to travel dangers on congested roads. Headlines are equally disheartening, such as the following:

"Highway collapse leaves at least 24 dead."

"Driver found guilty in fatal bus crash."

"Bridge accident plunge workers to their death."

"A Yellow Springs man was killed in a crash Thursday evening that injured three others, including two children."

"Beavercreek couple and child killed in a crash in Kentucky."

Devastating news about lives lost prematurely in road accidents continues to be heard every day. Some are preventable, particularly if they emanate from capricious actions.

It would have been a wide-sweeping tragedy to read a headline that says, "Professor and wife die in horrendous traffic accident on Lagos road." As much as we pray, t, these tragedies unfortunately still occur. Just as prevention is better than cure, it is a fact that preemption is better than redemption. We were saved and spared by our driver's fast reaction to evade the situation and prevent a potentially horrendous crash.

Our journey to Lagos Island started on the Mainland, Ikeja area, to be specific. Several family friends were invited to the august dinner reception in honor of the conclusion of the memorial lecture for the late Professor Oye Ibidapo-Obe at the University of Lagos campus. Professor Ibidapo-Obe had been a scholarly collaborator on a variety of intellectual engagements during his illustrious life. He died on January

3rd, 2021. Readers are referred to the Appendix of this book for my written tribute to Professor Ibidapo-Obe upon his demise. The second biennial memorial lecture, for which I was the keynote speaker took place on January 5th, 2024. The appreciation dinner, organized and hosted by his spouse, was scheduled for the 9th of January on the Victoria Island segment of the Lagos Island. This is why we were headed to the Island from the Mainland of Lagos. My wife and I had travelled to Nigeria, specifically for the memorial lecture. I had spoken remotely via Zoom at the first memorial lecture in 2022, but I had promised the family that I would attend the second memorial lecture in person.

We were just a few kilometres down the busy road to the Lagos Island. Everything looked smooth and safe. Our vehicle was on the outside lane, next to the concrete road median (or culvert), on a three-lane, right-hand-drive highway. Nothing looked out of the ordinary, until a pedestrian pushing a cart of construction iron, breached the concrete median and pushed his cart in front of our vehicle, with less than six feet of road to spare between us. Meanwhile, the traffic behind us was streaming along and bearing us from behind. At the same time, a large commercial trailer truck was on the right side of our vehicle, the passenger side. I was in the back seat on the passenger-side. My wife was in the back seat with me. She was seated on the driver-side of the vehicle. There was a split-second shout and reaction from our driver when this immense hazard suddenly interjected itself into the flow of traffic. The driver exclaimed in horror "Yehpa!!!" which is equivalent shouting "Oh God!" or (pardon the expression) "Shit!" While he exclaimed this unpleasant remark, he took an unbelievably evasive move, narrowly driving through the marginal space that existed between the loaded cart in front of us and the speeding truck on our right. It was like an angel lifted our vehicle through the clouds to avoid a horrific collision, which would have led to an extended pile up on the busy road. We were left visibly shaken in the back seat, full of praise for the driver's immaculate driving skills and thankful for God sparing our lives. Following this near-miss experience, we remained disoriented for many days to the extent that we cancelled all our subsequent trips to Lagos Island.

The Deji-vu story above is just one case example of what people experience directly in terms of a near-miss in traffic. There are countless similar and unrecognized near misses, dangers fitting this book's theme of the "margin of death." These can range the gamut, from petty crimes in the neighborhood that escalate to death-causing incidents to mass shootings and stabbings in public places. One such example is the testimony by a New York novelist, Paul Auster, who wrote about the "Element of Chance," in which case he narrowly missed being killed by lightening. According to his report, at the age of fourteen, he was at a summer camp, at which a boy next to him was struck and killed by lightening. His luck of the draw was that if the lightening had been just a few inches of over, it could have killed him instead. This was, indeed, a narrow margin of death. Sudden death became a preoccupation of Paul Auster's novels, based on his own observations.

On another front, the 2024 student protests that roiled university campuses in the USA were explosive enough in some cases that they could have led to someone's death. The paradox of life involves our extreme pursuits of enjoying life, only to create unrecognizable opportunities for untimely death. Death is a part of the cycle of life. The continuum of life, existence, and death can be unnerving, but it is the reality of life, itself. From a systems perspective, incidents that might, otherwise, appear to be innocuous, could lead to death. For example, the day the 911 emergency telephone system went out for over three hours in the USA states Nebraska, Nevada, South Dakota, and Texas. Millions of people lost the ability to reach out for emergency needs. Lives have been lost in the past in cases where 911 callers were not able to get emergency help when critically needed.

In another interesting testimony, I once saw a YouTube video where a husband wanted to play a practical joke on his wife by hiding under a pile of leaves raked from the Autumn foliage in the Midwest region of the USA. He claimed to enjoy playing harmless pranks on his wife. He timed his hideout to be just before his wife arrived home from work. The plan was for him to jump out of the pile of leaves as his wife walked by. He proudly announced, "I am going to jump out from under the pile of leaves and scare the crap out of her." Everything was going, according to plan, until the phone rang, and he prematurely jumped out of the pile of leaves to answer the phone call. Just as he was running towards his phone on a nearby bench, his wife came driving down the street and accelerated, deliberately, right through the pile of leaves because the pile was placed in front of the driveway of their home. Only seconds separated the barreling car from the man's fortuitous escape. The man narrowly escaped by some divine intervention. That's how the lucky man navigated through a narrow margin of death. In another series of videos, multiple pedestrians are shown narrowly missing disasters on many roadside accidents. Each case was a matter of inches of separation between death and survival. The caption on the videos says, "This is why you must pray every day." Yes, prayers do help from the perspective of positive thinking about desired outcomes, but what happens in the cases of those who, indeed, died from such accidents? Did they not pray fervently enough? My take on this "margin of death" theme is that, in addition to praying, we must take proactive actions to preempt disasters by being cautious of where disasters are likely to lurk.

In one personal testimony, my longtime childhood friend, Babs Ayeni, and I often recall our close call that we experienced while growing up in a neighborhood of Lagos, Nigeria. We were about ten years old then and we frequently played and pranked around the neighborhood, particularly in the afternoons after school. One day, we dared to challenge ourselves to jump in the Lagos river to demonstrate we could survive even though neither of us could swim at that time. The daring challenge was, fortuitously, overheard by an adult, who, forcefully, dissuaded us from trying what could have meant a sure death for both of us. We are both over 70 years old now, and we still get a kick out oof the stupidity that we almost embarked upon. The margin of death was narrowly averted by a passerby.

While remaining thankful for the road safety of Lagos on the 9th of January 2024, I am reminded of other moments of gratitude in relation to road incidents. Below is a recollection of how my family was rescued after our car broke down on the highways of Tennessee in the 1970s. The story of our mountain road rescue in Tennessee goes as re-narrated on the following pages.

Christmas stories often remind me of my family's experience in September 1977, on one of the imposing mountain roads on I-40 between Nashville and Cookeville, Tennessee. Our older son, Ade, was born on June 10th, 1977, and, as a part of our exploration of the USA during a late-Summer break from Tennessee Tech (before the Fall quarter of those days), we decided to drive our newly acquired jalopy car to New Orleans. It was a long, hard drive for relatively new foreign students and parents in the USA. Nonetheless, we had a good time and a memorable experience in Louisiana.

On the drive back, we were unable to make the long journey during daylight. We considered breaking the trip into two days, but we didn't have enough money to stay in a hotel somewhere enroute to home. We could not afford even the cheapest Motel 6 of those days. We decided to press on into the dark night. Things were going well until we were about twenty-five miles West of Cookeville. At around 10 p.m.,. our jalopy car, a high-mileage 1966 Ford Custom 500, needed to get us up and over the last test of endurance (the mountain in question, whose name I never knew). The car promptly conked out at a point that appeared to us (at that time) to be a perilous incline like we had never experienced before. We were scared, despondent, and worried about what could happen to us overnight in an unfamiliar area, where no one knew where we were, with a three-month old child on Iswat's lap. There were no laws about seatbelts and putting babies in car seats in those days.

There we were, a young black family of three, lost in the dark in an unknown Mountain location in Tennessee. It was, indeed, very terrifying. There was no exit nearby in the desolate and frightening bushes on either side of the road. There were no cell phones in those days. It was getting cold as mountain Winter was beginning to roll in at that time of the year. Sleeping in the car until we could get daylight help was not an option.

After several minutes of debating what to do next, I decided to step out of the car to see if my rudimentary, yet unproven and untested, engineering skills could assist us in fixing our situation. I knew I could not do anything, but as the head of the family, I thought I should demonstrate that I was, at least, trying to do something. I opened the hood, groped in the dark for one wire or another, and silently prayed that the Hands of God would guide me to the right wire that would magically bring the car to life. Nothing happened.

Meanwhile, all sorts of paired lights whizzed by, despite the 55 mph Interstate speed limit of those days. Blowing torrents of high-powered air that rocked the disabled car and its occupants. Some of the passing lights were high while some were low. Since I could not make out the outlines of the vehicles, I could only guess their varying sizes. The hood was up, the darkness was unforgiving, and Iswat could not see me or what I was doing. Due to the ambient noise of the passing interstate traffic, I could only faintly hear her calling out to me, hoping that I would have an answer. I had none and offered her no response. Besides, my lips were beginning to quiver due to the descending cold of the night and I could hardly speak.

Worried about my welfare, she stepped out of the car with Ade in her arms. She stood beside me on the road-marker side of the road shoulder as if to shield me from the vehicles zooming past our car. I continued to fidget under the hood as if knew what I was doing. Suddenly, a pair of lights that had been approaching fast suddenly slowed down and went a few yards past our location before reversing toward us.

Judging by the height of the lights off the ground, I guessed this must be a large car. We did not know what to make of it. *Are they coming to help us or kill us?* I questioned in my mind. Of course, I did not reveal the latter of those two thoughts to Iswat. I softly said, "Maybe we will get some help from them."

When the car got close enough to us, it stopped. A big elderly man and a young lady came out of the car; the man from the driver side, and lady from the passenger side of the back seat. The man started saying "Do you need . . . . .?" but before he could get in another word, he was interrupted by the young lady, who appeared to be about eighteen or nineteen years old. She exclaimed to the older man, "Dad, he is my classmate at Tech, we need to help them." I was shocked. This lady was definitely not in any of my classes at Tennessee Tech. She then asked me, "Are you going back to Cookeville? That's where my parents are taking me back to school." How she guessed that we were going to Cookeville, I never knew. It could have been because she immediately knew that we were foreign individuals, obviously of college age, and could only be heading toward the university town of Cookeville. I quickly said "Yes."

The young lady then turned to Iswat to ask, "How are you and your baby?" Iswat nodded her positive affirmation and then the young lady said, "We can give you a ride because Tennessee Tech is where we are going." I replied, "Thank you, we live at Tech Village," the university housing for married Tennessee Tech students. Nodding her head in the direction of her father, the young lady appeared more excited by saying "they are taking me to my residence hall at Tech." Meanwhile, the father had no chance to say anything. The young lady did all the talking and negotiation. Leaving all our travel items in our disabled car, we hopped in the back seat of the large car and sat beside the young lady, who resumed her previous seating location in the car. An older lady was in the front passenger seat. She politely greeted us and welcomed us into the car. The car pulled back out onto the Interstate and we happily rode with this unknown family toward Cookeville.

It was during the ride that we learned what prompted the family to stop to help us in the first place. The young lady was moved by the sight of seeing someone holding a baby on the side of the Interstate in such a cold, dark, and deserted location. She urged her parents to stop and help. Based on that account, I concluded that in her sympathetic urge to help, she must have lied to her parents, on the spur of the moment, that she recognized me as a classmate. It was the greatest helpful lie ever told. I was further convinced of this because the young lady did most of the talking and never once mentioned anything about the class that we were, supposedly, taking together. If she was my classmate, she would have mentioned something about our class together.

Stunned by the family's unsolicited help, Iswat and I kept quiet throughout the twenty-five-mile drive, except for occasional responses to inquisitive questions posed by the young lady and the older lady. "What is your baby's name?" "Where did you travel to?" "How long did you drive?" On we went until we were dropped off at our Tech Village apartment. We thanked them and bade them farewell. Iswat and I had arrived in the USA from Nigeria only two years prior, and we did not ask for the names of the family. In our culture, which we still find difficult to pull away from, it is an extreme disrespect to ask an older person for his or her name. What are you going to do with the name? Call the person by name? That's a big no, no. Thus, we never learned anything about this very generous and caring family. The family probably voluntarily offered their names, but we did not remember in our moment of anxiety. This is something I still regret until today.

Very early the next morning, Mr. Bassey Udosen, one of the other Nigerian students at Tennessee Tech, and I went in his car to attempt to rescue and retrieve my disabled car. Mr. Udosen was a Mechanical Engineering student and was well versed in tinkering with mechanical things. We got to my car and it was still intact. All our travel items were still in it. It appeared to be none the worse for wear. Not trusting what would happen, I opened the door, inserted the ignition key, and cranked the engine.

Miraculously, the car roared to life without any other prompting. It must have been driven long and hard the previous day to the point of exhaustion. It was not the radiator because that would have signaled its distress with a flash of steam or fire. I drove the car back to Cookeville without any incident. Mr. Bassey Udosen followed me in his own car to ensure that mine did not pull any other surprises. I arrived home safe and sound. Thus, we ended the harrowing experience with a Jalopy Car. We never took another long trip in that car for as long as we owned it. We remain eternally thankful for the help offered to us by the nameless family. The preceding story is composed in a thankful recollection. Had we not been rescued by the gracious family, we could have, perhaps, faced a precarious margin of God knows what.

Related to social linkages are cases where the neglect of social responsibilities could lead to criminal activities that could lead to someone's death. Such margins of death exist in many communities and should not be taken for granted. I once wrote about this type of community linkage in a short piece in the past. The socially focused essay is echoed below as a social responsibility commentary of why community wingman ship should be every day for everyone. We are all in the same pot of a social mess. When the pot is stirred, we all end up in the messy mix; and what goes around comes back around to touch every one of us. It is the responsibility of each us to act and make contributions in early stages to preempt bigger social problems and prevent being personally touched by socially derailing crimes later on.

The report of a past Florida school shooting brings up an important issue and the necessity for community wingman ship. Mass shootings in schools, churches, meetings, offices, and what have you. It is a sad epoch of human existence. The recurrence of these acts of violence points to the need for more wingman ship efforts toward everyone every day. This is important, not just within the military, but also within society. Our lives are more intertwined than we want to believe. What goes around in one place comes around everywhere else. Whenever a horrific act like this happens, we clamor for one remedy or another, including more gun control. However, that is just one piece of the system of systems of remedies. One aspect that is often ignored is the need for earlier watchfulness and preemptive wingman ship. We need to direct more efforts toward preemptive measures that can prevent mass violence. We often ask for the motive of such an act. Of course, we never know for sure, but one thing that is clear is that feelings of despondency can lead a person toward a disregard for life, of self and of others. The military ethos and culture of wingman ship, if applied broadly within the external community, has a lot to offer in terms of helping everyone develop a feeling of belonging.

In this context, wingman ship is everyone's social responsibility and should be practiced daily. There is a need for everyone to take on the social responsibility for everyone else, particularly the youth. The adage that "it takes a village to raise a child" has never been truer than in the present days of social uncertainties. Social stability and advancement of our society is everyone's responsibility. We cannot afford to look the other way whenever we notice something that is not right or does not support the welfare of society. Social issues that we fail to address now may magnify into incidents that could adversely touch everyone in society, directly or indirectly. As individuals, we owe it to ourselves and our community to participate in the resolution of societal problems actively and directly. There is so much decadence evolving in modern society. Many of these deplorable social issues manifest themselves in the form of criminal activities brought on by feelings of frustration, disenfranchisement, isolation, depression, desperation, and hopelessness. When members of our community are noted to be facing mental stress, financial discomfort, and despondency, it should behoove all of us to offer helping hands. The extension of help can preempt serious problems later. If we do not help, minor problems may turn into felonious incidents that can come back to touch us in unanticipated ways.

A community may think it is safe by cocooning itself within the secure walls of its neighborhood, but the reality is that no one can be completely insulated from problems that occur within the community. With freedom of movement and closing of geographical gaps, crime importation and exportation should be a big concern for everyone. We should all share in the collective responsibility of helping to preempt the evolution of social decadence so that we don't have to deal with the results later.

It is obvious that prisons have become a huge drain on society. Whether we want to accept it or not, we all pay for prisons. We pay in terms of loss of human capital, loss of loved ones, impedance of economic growth, and the opportunity cost of the loss of a productive workforce. Wouldn't it have been cheaper to institute programs that would preempt criminal tendencies and, consequently, reduce the need for more prisons? For social ills, preemption is far better than incarceration. Programs that help to forestall crime are often cheap, subtle, and innocuous; such as offering social support to the less fortunate, providing a basis for optimism in youth, creating an atmosphere of belonging for everyone, offering encouragement, projecting empathy, and facilitating educational opportunities. For youth, support, discipline, and comfort are as much a responsibility of the parents as they are of everyone in the community. We are not all too far removed from the possible adverse impacts of juvenile delinquency. Education and support systems are sure ingredients for advancing society and minimizing criminal acts and horrific incidents. We should all practice wingman ship every single day of every year toward everyone.

Another interesting story from my Deji-Vu collection is my fictional encounter with a tree. As much as we adore and admire trees, sometimes an encounter with one could be deadly, fitting the definition of a margin of death.

The USA Occupational Safety and Health Administration (OSHA) reports that on average, there are over 100 landscape and **tree-related** fatalities every year. Within the tree care industry, these numbers are even higher. In fact, the tree care industry is one of the most dangerous in America. In a Philadelphia blog not long ago, the law firm Reiff presents an opinion that of all nature's flora and fauna, trees seem to be among the very safest. After all, trees cannot sting or bite us. They can't lay eggs in our floorboards, or peck and scratch at our vulnerable flesh. They can't infect open wounds or bite down on our ankles and drag us beneath the surface of the ocean. They seem harmlessly anchored deep in the ground, still and serene for all time. However, while it's true that trees are perfectly safe in the vast majority of instances, it *is* possible for trees to pose a danger along the line of a margin of death. It may be a bizarre accident which can only be attributed to natural forces or a matter of negligent maintenance involving carelessness and liability.

It was mid-July, the height of the typical rainy season in Tennessee. I had gone to an administrative meeting and was walking back to my office along a tree-lined pathway. A beautiful, tall, eastward leaning tree caught my attention. I looked at the tree suspiciously. Something was playing mysteriously in my subconscious mind. The evening news the previous night had reported several downed trees in my neighborhood because of the prior thunderstorms. My mind must have been wondering innocently why this tree was still standing despite the abuse it must have suffered over the years. As I walked past the tree, I eyed it curiously but cautiously, as if to say, "I'm watching you." Suddenly, the tree started to fall in my direction as if my suspicious stare instigated a retaliatory action from the tree. I froze instantly. This was due to two reasons that I did not appreciate at the time.

One half of my immobilization was due to fright. The other half must have been due to my quick assessment of the situation at hand. It is amazing how quickly the mind races through thoughts in moments like this. Thoughts and rationalization that would have taken hours to untangle quickly became clear. While still standing frozen, I thought if I moved too soon, the tree would figure out my intention and it would change its course to come after me viciously. I waited until the split second when I knew the tree could no longer change its falling course and I jumped away from it. In my younger and more pliable days, I would have jumped at least six feet off the tree's course, but my limbs have lost much of their elasticity in recent years., I only managed to land a couple of feet away. Soon after, the tree smashed into the ground. Although the main trunk missed me, I could not escape the malicious lashings of the branches. Flashes of the lashes that those in medieval servitude must have felt came to my mind. What a terrible ordeal.

I sheepishly picked myself up from the ground after being sent on my knees by the "crazy" branches. Long and telling streaks of open flesh lined my body. I asked myself, *How am I going to explain to anyone that a tree did this to me?* My wife certainly would not believe me. She has always accused me of telling tales because I am an imaginative writer. My children would surely find this amusing. I have always chastised them not to get into any whipping encounters. "Avoid troubles so that you don't come home with scratches. It would seem that I have not lived up to my parental preaching in this situation. I thought of hiding until all the evidence had healed but that would not work. I was expected home soon, and I would risk close inspection once my tattered clothing was noticed. I thought of going to the store and buying new coveralls, but that would not work either because it was a hot summer and coveralls were the opposite of my normal summer attire. Finally, I concluded that the right thing to do was tell the truth. Everyone would be understanding and supportive once they heard my plight. I thought I would put a humorous start to the story to put listeners into a good sympathetic mood. So, upon getting home, I told my wife how a tree beat me into a pulp. Her terse response was that I should have been sucked into the pulp of the tree. So much for a compassionate companion. To make a long story short, I did not get the domicile sympathy that I deserved and anticipated. To be tongue-lashed after being tree-lashed is quite humiliating. I'll have to watch out more closely for falling trees next time. For their own part, the leaning trees are watching me, ever more ominously.

No one ever knows the margin of death when a travel schedule is delayed. We are often disappointed (or even mad) when a flight is delayed or cancelled. Who knows what could have happened if the original travel schedule was maintained.

Here is an example that starts with an innocuous announcement.

"If you're on Flight 881 going to Knoxville, we've just been notified of a ten-minute delay," the muttering of an outer-space alien voice announced over the airport intercom. Voices coming from far-off alien space often reach Earth distorted.

"Sir, what did she just announce?" I asked a fellow flier, who seemed to be a seasoned Cosmo traveler himself.

"The tower just announced a ten-minute delay," he reassured me.

"That's not bad," I opined. With the *good* weather we're having, I was expecting worse . . . . like a one-hour delay.

Ten minutes later, I walked over to the counter, "Are we going to be taking off soon? It's been more than five minutes past the original ten minutes announced earlier," I inquired with subdued humility. The counter, in its inanimate best, reiterated the earlier reassurance that we would be taking off soon.

Thirty minutes later, the inevitable was announced. Another five to ten more minutes. *Okay, I can deal with that*, I thought. The announcer continued, "We'll get you there as fast and safely as we can." Yah, that air of safety concern that soothes and pacifies irate passengers. We all kept quiet, seemingly lethargic to the incremental announcements.

One hour later, I summoned enough courage, and walked over to the counter again. "Are we making progress toward departure?" This inquisitive query elicited an account of the source of the delay in a whisper. "We don't want to panic passengers or anything like that, but the pilot is arriving on another flight coming in from Frankfurt. We'll depart as soon as he rushes through immigration and customs." Poor fellow! He will have to race from the international concourse to get to the regional wing just to make sure we are not delayed any longer. He will be all ruffled up, probably sweaty from the intra-airport run.

Finally, thirty minutes later, the pilot arrived, walked briskly to the counter, showed his badge, and was waved onto the aisle leading to the cockpit. I watched him closely, monitored his relaxed strides, and marveled at his quick recovery from a stressful intercontinental flight and the dash from gate to gate.

Anticipating departure, I packed up my belongings that had, by now, worked their ways onto adjacent seats, creating a defensive buffer between me and neighboring passengers. Nothing happened for several more minutes.

Thankfully, we boarded twenty minutes later.

"Welcome aboard," a flight attendant announced. "This flight is completely full, make sure all your belongings fit in the overhead bins and please sit in your own seat. We're so full that you will not be able to change seats on this flight." We all complied. Being a self-imposed compliant conformist, I reined in all my wayward belongings and made room for my in-bound seat mate.

Now comfortable, I shut my eyes and dozed off. The backward jerk of the plane woke me up as my packed-in elbow flayed uncontrollably into the next seat. "Excuse me, ... I am sorry," I murmured in my sleep-induced stupor. My seat mate did not respond. I opened my eyes, turned my head to make apologetic eye contact. I saw right through him straight onto the next row of seats. Just then, the flight attendant, all primed up like a flying angel, came down the aisle.

Packing in my shoulders to signify my earlier compliance, I asked her, "Where's my seat mate? I made room for him you know." She looked intently into my eyes and just snickered.

I got the message . . . . it's all a pack of airtight lies.

In multiple scholarly journal publications, authors have addressed many reasons for traffic accidents, as summarized below. Every year, road accidents claim the lives of millions of people and cause countless injuries worldwide. These accidents not only result in personal tragedies but also impose a heavy economic burden on individuals, families, and society as a whole.

Insurance companies have vested interests in minimizing road accidents and reducing their liabilities. Studies by insurance companies have resulted in tips and guidelines for reducing accidents. While accidents can occur due to various factors, it is crucial to understand the auto insurance components of responding to road accidents, thereby promoting safer driving habits and mitigating risks. Insurance companies have delved into the most prevalent causes of road accidents and the ensuing insurance implications. For this reason, it is important for city planners and leaders to have good road policies in place to make cities, desirably, more "wreckless." Along this line, a law in Ohio prohibits newly-licensed teens from driving without parental supervision between 9 p.m. and 6 a.m.

According to a release by a coalition of European insurance companies, some common causes of accidents are summarized in the paragraphs that follow.

Distracted Driving

In recent years, distracted driving has become one of the leading causes of road accidents. With the proliferation of smartphones and other electronic devices, drivers are increasingly tempted to engage in activities like texting, talking on the phone, checking social media, or even watching videos while behind the wheel. These distractions divert their attention from the road and significantly increase the chances of an accident.

Speeding

Excessive speed is a major contributor to road accidents. When drivers exceed the speed limits, they compromise their ability to react to sudden changes in road conditions, increase the braking distance required, and reduce the effectiveness of vehicle control. Speeding not only endangers the driver's life but also puts other road users at risk.

Drunk Driving

Driving under the influence of alcohol or drugs remains a significant cause of road accidents. Intoxicated drivers experience impaired judgment, reduced reaction times, and decreased coordination, all of which makes them highly susceptible to causing accidents. The solution to this problem lies in responsible behavior, which means refraining from driving after consuming alcohol or taking any substance that impairs one's ability to operate a vehicle safely.

Reckless Driving

Reckless driving encompasses a range of dangerous behaviors on the road, including aggressive maneuvers, tailgating, running red lights, and changing lanes without signaling. Such reckless actions often lead to collisions and severe injuries. Practicing defensive driving techniques, which involve anticipating and responding to potential hazards, is crucial in avoiding accidents caused by reckless drivers.

Poor Weather Conditions

Inclement weather conditions such as heavy rain, snow, fog, or ice make roads slippery and decrease visibility, significantly increasing the likelihood of accidents. These adverse conditions require drivers to adapt their driving techniques accordingly. Slowing down, increasing the following distance, and ensuring adequate visibility. The use of lights and wipers are essential precautions to prevent accidents caused by poor weather conditions. Additionally, staying informed about weather forecasts and planning travel accordingly can help minimize exposure to hazardous weather.

According to some car insurance coalition releases, despite taking precautionary measures, accidents can still occur due to various factors. Precaution is an ultimate path to better road protection and survival. In such unfortunate events, having adequate insurance coverage can provide financial protection and peace of mind. Car insurance policies cover damages to the insured vehicle, medical expenses, and liabilities arising from accidents. It is crucial to select a policy that suits individual needs and preferences, considering factors such as coverage limits, deductibles, and additional benefits like roadside assistance or rental car reimbursement.

According to auto insurance companies, understanding the common causes of road accidents is essential for promoting safer driving practices and reducing the risks associated with travelling on dangerous roads. By recognizing the dangers of distracted driving, speeding, drunk driving, reckless behavior, and other risk factors, individuals can adopt responsible driving habits that prioritize road safety. Citizens are encouraged to practice more responsible driving. Some guidelines provided by insurance companies are summarized below:

1. **What should I do if I encounter a distracted driver on the road?**

    If you notice a driver who appears distracted, it is important to maintain a safe distance from their vehicle and avoid any aggressive actions. Focus on your own driving, be cautious, and give the distracted driver plenty of space. If necessary, you can report the incident to local law enforcement with details such as the license plate number, location, and a description of the vehicle.

2. **How can I prevent accidents caused by poor weather conditions?**

To prevent accidents caused by poor weather conditions, it is crucial to adjust your driving behavior accordingly. Reduce your speed, increase the following distance between vehicles, and use headlights and windshield wipers appropriately. Stay informed about weather forecasts before travelling, and if the conditions are severe, consider postponing your trip if possible.

3. **What should I do if I suspect a driver is under the influence of alcohol or drugs?**

If you suspect a driver is impaired by alcohol or drugs, do not attempt to confront or engage with them directly. Instead, keep a safe distance and promptly contact local law enforcement, providing them with as much information as possible, including the vehicle's description, license plate number, and the location and direction of travel. Reporting such incidents can help prevent potential accidents and protect other road users.

4. What role does defensive driving play in preventing accidents caused by reckless behavior?

Defensive driving is a crucial skill that helps anticipate and respond to potential hazards on the road. By practicing defensive driving, you can better identify and avoid reckless behavior exhibited by other drivers. It involves maintaining a safe following distance, being attentive to your surroundings, and being prepared to react quickly and safely to unexpected situations.

5. How can I handle an encounter with wildlife while driving?

If you encounter wildlife on the road, it is essential to stay calm and avoid sudden movements or swerving, which can cause a loss of control. Slow down and honk your horn to alert the animals, giving them an opportunity to move away. If a collision with wildlife is unavoidable, prioritize your safety and try to minimize the impact by braking firmly and maintaining control of your vehicle.

Workforce Protection and Preservation

Since we are talking about the subject of the loss of lives in traffic wrecks, I want to point out that a loss through any means is still a loss. Each person that is lost is a vital component of the local workforce. We should be concerned about all losses in the workforce, regardless of the way the losses occur. I am passionate about protecting and preserving all members of the workforce. So, I present my strong views about this in the following paragraphs.

Workforce preservation has been a focus of interest of mine for many years. The interest arises from the realization that untimely deaths, due to accidents or nefarious human activities, rob a nation of its vital human resources. One of my past writings in this is reprinted here, specifically in the context of workforce development and preservation for national renewable energy strategies and implementation, for the case of Capacity Building needs for the proactive adoption of renewable energy and energy efficiency in Nigeria.

As the nation of Nigeria is now worrying and agitating about the future of energy in the country, with a particular focus on switching to renewable energy, it helps to remind ourselves of the long-ago quote by Winston Churchill:

"Let our advance worrying become
advance thinking and planning."
– Winston Churchill

This quote was uttered in the wake of World War II, worry that pervaded the entire world. What we are facing these days is akin to a world war on the future of energy. The Renewable Energy Committee of the Nigerian Academy of

Engineering (NAE – Nigeria) has been tasked to ruminate and strategize on how the nation could develop strategies for moving towards renewable energy. Among several topics being tackled by the committee, members of the committee are specifically charged with addressing the topic of "Capacity Building Needs for the Active Adoption of Renewable Energy and Energy Efficiency in Nigeria." Therein lies my submission tendered herewith.

I have focused on workforce preservation in Nigeria (and elsewhere) because of an unfortunate incident that I witnessed in Nigeria in 2000 (See Attachment I). My approach to contributing in this regard leverages a rarely addressed theme of workforce preservation. Workforce, in this sense, relates to "manpower development or capacity building" in the usual parlance of developing nations. My argument in this approach centers on the need to not only "build capacity," but also "preserve capacity." If you build capacity, you must preserve it for it to provide a meaningful result for the nation. People constitute the primary capacity of a nation. Thus, any effort about building capacity must also address a commitment to preserving (i.e., keeping safe) capacity (i.e., people) that has been developed. Whatever the strategy might be for transitioning to renewable energy, people will, ultimately, be responsible for implementing the strategy. What happens if the people educated, trained, and groomed to lead the renewable energy initiative are not available to execute the charge due to being vanquished by a lack of safety and security in the nation. We often make the mistake of believing that highly trained personnel (e.g., engineers, policy makers, decision makers, managers, movers, and shakers) will always be there and available to deliver the goals and objectives of renewable energy. This is a fallacy, as my testimony narrated fully in Attachment I would reveal. The genesis of the testimony is that I witnessed the life of a highly educated professional being taken due to an incident of armed robbery. I came to the realization that all efforts to educate, train, and prepare this professional for national development went for nothing, all because his life could not be preserved. For all of us, no matter how Interested, Willing, and Available (IWA) we think we are, our lives could be in jeopardy in a flash, if safety and security are not assured. Please read Attachment I to get the full background story of my approach to this strategy-development task.

Too often, we focus too much on the provision of technology (e.g., ICT: Information and Communications Technology) to get things done. Unfortunately, we often neglect the process and the people involved. If the process is flawed and the people are not protected and preserved, no technology can solve our problem. The nexus of achieving goals and objectives in renewable energy and other pursuits revolves around technology, people, and process. People, as the constituents of the workforce, are essential and must be preserved. We should invest in renewable energy workforce development and preserve the people constituting the workforce for renewable energy.

There is an urgent need to broaden the national communication channels related to renewable energy programs and initiatives. Most often, we (engineers, researchers, professors, and intellectuals) preach to the choir among ourselves. Rarely do we engage with the public on the issues of renewable energy, its importance, and relevance to our general wellbeing and future survival. The public represents the bulk of the population required to adopt renewable energy practices. However we rarely engage the public in public-service and public-awareness programs to promote renewable energy. Here, I present my Triple C (communication, cooperation, and coordination) framework for getting everyone on board for project goals and objectives. This framework is recommended for the nationwide push towards renewable energy. The Nigerian Academy of Engineering can step forward to be the conduit for sensitizing the public to the benefits and urgency of converting to renewable energy. Badiru (2024) leverages the Triple C framework for pushing efforts to reengineer our actions to influence our environmental world positively. Increasing participation through direct involvement will pay dividends in having more people to embrace renewable energy more broadly. The lesson from Confucius is applicable here, as echoed in the quote below:

"Tell me, and I forget;
Show me, and I remember;
Involve me, and I understand."
– Confucius (Chinese)

The more we communicate the terms and requirements of road safety to the public, the more people can get involved, and the better they can understand. In this regard, bi-directional communication pathways will embrace bottom-up and top-down communication streams. Clear communication leads to personal cooperation, which leads to the coordination of individual actions. The theme of this framework is to inform the audience of the value and benefit of road safety. Some pertinent questions that can be included in the Triple-C framework of road safety include the following:

- What is the purpose of?
- What exactly is required of each participant?
- Why is communication required?
- What is the urgency of road safety initiatives?
- Who oversees the national drive for road safety?
- What is the cost of promoting road safety?
- Who will bear the cost?
- How is an ordinary consumer going to participate in road safety?

Communication should be bi-directional, covering the different stakeholders, including federal level, state level, local level, institutional level, community level, company level, neighborhood level, household level, and personal level. The flow of communication should be embraced.

This section is an adaptation of one of my workforce-centric articles, with a refocused emphasis on the current era of workforce development, as it might relate to renewable energy programs post-COVID-19. The workforce disruption caused by COVID-19 necessitated a new focus on the challenges of workforce development around the world. The decimation of productive human resources caused by COVID-19 requires not only the traditional strategies of workforce development, but also the uncharted territory of workforce redevelopment and preservation. The reports we are getting indicate a precipitous decline in the ability of the workforce to continue to contribute to economic development and vitality of a nation. When businesses opened back up, it was necessary for workers to adapt to the changes brought forward by the pandemic. Once adapted to these changes, workers aimed to return to the level of proficiency and efficiency that was needed to keep the economy moving forward. The technical topic of learning curve analysis postulates that performance improves with repeated cycles of operations. Whenever work performance is interrupted for a prolonged period, as we experienced during COVID-19, the processes of natural forgetting or technical regressing set in. To offset this decline, direct concerted efforts must be made beyond anything we have experienced before. This led to our call for new innovations in workforce development and redevelopment. We cannot be lackadaisical in leaving things to the normal process of regaining form, routine, and function. In the present era, return-to-work programs should consider efforts to reorganize for renewable energy, particularly related to the mode and frequency of transportation. Work-at-home programs may alter renewable energy practices. It is the recommendation of this section that rigorous research and policy studies be conducted within the context of workforce interfaces for renewable energy.

Typically, we erroneously focus on technical tools as the embodiment of workforce development. More often than not, process innovations might be just as vital. Workforce development is more of a process development than of a tool development. There are numerous human factors that can enhance the goals of workforce development. Some of the innovations recommended here include paying attention to the hierarchy of needs of the worker, recognizing the benefits of diversity, elevating the visibility of equity, instituting efforts to negate adverse aspects of cultural bias, and appreciating the dichotomy of socio-economic infrastructure. While not too expensive to implement, these innovative strategies can be tremendously effective in the push for renewable energy. To tie this to the earlier discussion of workforce preservation, it should be noted that safety is one of the critical needs of the workforce. Safety, as earlier argued, directly impacts workforce preservation. A workforce member eliminated by a COVID, or other safety-related incidents, is a workforce member that we fail to preserve. Typically, society addresses safety and security as necessary social mandates. My recommendation here is that we need to elevate that perception to the level of workforce necessity for workforce preservation.

As one cliché emanating from the COVID-19 pandemic has taught us, "we are all in this together." To this end, we must all reengineer our actions for the purpose of advancing workforce development, such that renewable energy initiatives could take hold. A skilled workforce is the cornerstone of national development. However, the pursuit of manpower development without measures of preservation is analogous to building a national foundation on quicksand. Without risking a loss of generality, let us accept "manpower" as an idiosyncratic term referring to both men and women. For this reason, I often use "manpower" and "workforce" interchangeably. All sectors of the Nigerian economy proclaim their dedication to workforce development with the fervor of a trumpeter. Nowhere is it ever mentioned that workforce preservation is just as important as its development. Workforce development without a preservation strategy symbolizes a non-holistic view. Without a preservation strategy, any development effort is bound to fail. The neglect of workforce preservation pervades both the public and private sectors; and it is obvious that the neglect of preservation strategies is one reason that our national development continues to flutter. For Nigeria to advance, there must be an urgent development of a strategy to preserve whatever workforce is developed.

I have had opportunities to participate in various workforce development initiatives in Nigeria over the past two decades. During all the strategic deliberations, not once was workforce preservation mentioned as a co-requisite for workforce development. A recent tragic event instigated my urge to write on this issue at the time. Many concerned citizens have written and offered suggestions about policies and actions needed to solve pervasive problems in Nigeria. There is no shortage of ideas. There is no shortage of passionate and eloquent solution strategies. What is lacking is the will, ability, and dedication to implement the solutions. For this reason, I, at first, hesitated to write this article. I did not want to clutter the newsprint with yet another set of grandiose ideas devoid of action. However, this case is significant enough that I can risk grandiosity, with the hope that some action might follow. As a concerned citizen, I see it as my obligation to bring this plight to the attention of other citizens. Every one of us knows of at least one "developed" workforce that has been brutally eliminated from the nation's workforce pool. Thus, leaving a long train of family agony and national deprivation. We can hardly imagine the level of opportunity cost incurred because of the lost workforce. I suspect that some of the difficulties faced in revitalizing some sectors of the economy may be due to the frequent loss of trained, developed, experienced, and valuable workforce. We all recognize burnout as a national concern. Permanent workforce burnout is more devastating. This reality, unfortunately, receives less attention.

The case in point mentioned earlier in this section is that of the late Mr. Al-Hassan Alasa, who was recently cruelly eliminated from the nation's workforce pool by armed robbers. Mr. Alasa might not have been a celebrity in the usual sense of the word, but in my mind, he was a public figure, whose case deserves widespread public knowledge. Nigeria lost a gem of a gentleman.

I met Mr. Alasa at a training session at TCC (Training and Conference Center) Ogere. He made such an impression on me during the first few minutes that I felt as if I had known him for a long time. We discussed, among other things, technical workforce needs in Nigeria, changes in society, democracy, political and business advancements in Nigeria, as well as the new banking systems in Nigeria. We discussed the new service initiatives available at his bank (Standard Bank and Trust). He pointed me to the bank's new website, which I subsequently enjoyed visiting. Banking, Mr. Alasa's profession, has advanced tremendously in the past few years since the crop of professionals, like Mr. Alasa, came into the industry. If his life hadn't been cruelly taken away, he would have made far more contributions to the banking industry and the nation. Unfortunately, the people of the underworld did not allow him. What a waste of a national resource!

I was so distraught about Mr. Alasa's death that I was not myself for several days. I kept hoping that the sudden news would turn out to be a hoax. To my chagrin, the news checked out after I reconfirmed with another mutual friend of ours. I had innocently sent him an email, not realizing that the forced hand of death had descended upon him. Being away from the country, I had not heard the news about his encounter with armed robbers. After several weeks of not hearing back from him, I inquired from an acquaintance of his. Thus, came the sad news. I can only imagine what this loss would have meant to his family, his co-workers, his industry, and all those who had the good fortune to have known him. It is a devastating loss to everyone, a lingering pain.

Mr. Alasa's case is one of many cases that combine to remind us how fragile the pillars of workforce development could be. Several organizations spend millions for personnel security within and around company premises. What happens beyond company premises is an arrant display of insecurity. Workforce assets that are preserved while at work become vulnerable in the open community. Many valuable employees are lost during tragic encounters on the roads. To make matters worse, prospective workforce pools are cruelly mauled down before they can be cultivated.

New (even radical) approaches may have to be explored to preserve our workforce assets. One strategy that is worthy of consideration is the pooling of security resources to provide a blanket of protection for citizens at work, on the road, and at home. This essentially requires always making the nation safe for all. I refer to this concerted effort as Security Synergy, which provides a more effective security program than the individualized and localized efforts of separate organizations.

National security, personal safety, and personnel preservation are essential for a sustainable national development. How can security synergy be achieved nationwide? This will require voluntary and consensus agreement among companies. Strategic communication, cooperation, and coordination are the hallmark of developing and maintaining national safety for the purpose of workforce preservation. If the business environment is safe, the business climate will be stable, and companies can thrive and contribute to national development programs.

A voluntary security levy or corporate donation can be solicited and dedicated to the provision of an integrated security program under the auspices of existing national security forces, but under the trusteeship of a committee of company security representatives. This will help mitigate the frequent complaints about lack of governmental resources to provide adequate security. Why should companies embrace this sort of additional burden on their meagre revenue base? Well, it is a matter of interest in workforce preservation and cost effectiveness. Preservation of a trained workforce makes economic sense for a company. In addition, pooling of security resources, if carefully orchestrated and managed, can provide more widespread benefit for all; thereby, reducing the risk and burden associated with individualized programs.

The memory of lost loved ones, such as the late Al-Hassan Alasa, necessitates that we act on workforce preservation and minimize the adverse impacts of the margin of death. May God give us the strength to pursue the correct solutions.

DRIVING SENSES AND CENTS

Now that we have covered the topic of possible death from road accidents, we can move on to some driving-specific details. Driving requires the full attention and complete situational awareness of the driver, in ways that highlight the cost implications. Cost, in this case, could be in terms of financial cost as well as loss of life. The "cents" component in the title of this chapter relates to the multi-dimensional cost implications of traffic accidents. This could come in terms of repair cost, car rental cost, higher insurance premium, and/or the cost of not having a vehicle. The antidote for avoiding the unpleasant cost implications is to go "wreckless" in traffic engagements.

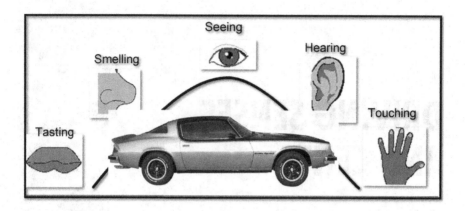

All five human senses must be engaged in the process of driving and staying safe on the road. Seeing, hearing, tasting, touching, smelling, and verbalizing are all essential in having a safe driving experience. Sometimes we talk about having the sixth sense. In the summation of this section of this book, "common sense" could be viewed as the sixth sense. Common sense could be the overriding asset that could be coupled with the other senses to ensure better road safety so that we can go wreckless in the city and beyond.

Sense of Taste

It might appear that the sense of taste does not have a direct correlation to driving. I opine that it does. If while driving, you suddenly have a sensation of a particular taste in your mouth, it behooves you to pay attention to it. It could be a medical issue. It could be toxic incursion into the driving space. It could be a sip of a contraband liquid that deceivingly appears to be ordinary water.

Sense of Smell

Smell can represent a warning of something burning in the vicinity of the driving engagement. A strong smell of burning rubber could be an indication of a brake-pad problem from the vehicle, your own or a different one.

Sense of Sight

This is the most obvious asset for driving. This is why drivers must keep their eyes on the road. Always pay attention and keep all critical views unobstructed. Make use of available rear-view and side-view mirrors. Keep your eyes sharp and keen through proper and regular vision checkups.

Sense of Hearing

Hearing is very important in ensuring safe driving habits. The ability to hear traffic sounds, alerts, and warning honks is necessary for avoiding disasters and going wreckless. The evolution of quieter engines in vehicles has elicited some worries. Overly silent vehicles could cause an accident and the proverbial excuse of "that vehicle came out of nowhere." Of course, all vehicles come from somewhere, whether or not you see or hear them. The concern about driving silence is the reason some automakers "force" some level of noise into the operation of their vehicles. Many motorcycles are deliberately designed to be noisy so they can be heard, if not seen in heavy and fast-moving traffic. The evolving prevalence of quiet electric vehicles is raising more worries and concerns in this regard. Silent vehicles can creep up on pedestrians and cause accidents.

Sense of Touch

Touch and feel are important in driving. This is particularly crucial in manual-transmission vehicles, which are still very common in Europe. The ability to reach out, touch, and operate the gear-shift mechanism (without looking) is useful for safe driving.

Common Sense

As I have emphasized earlier and repeatedly, common sense, rules over driving habits and desires. Common sense, along with intelligence, skills, and self-discipline, constitute the prerequisites for complying with the physics of safe driving for the purpose of going wreckless in the city and beyond. Drivers must exercise common sense regardless of the other driving assets that are in effect. For example, if you make your intention known, 80% of other drivers will let you have your way. No need to cut in abruptly and cause a wreck.

The Cents of It All

The dollars and cents of safe driving can be conveyed through the enormous costs from the loss of lives and other concomitant expenses. Some costs are:

- Auto insurance.
- Auto registration.
- Vehicle service and fees.
- Driving assessments within large and crowed cities.
- Road maintenance.
- Fuel for operating vehicles.

In 2024, it is reported that 294 million vehicles are registered in the USA. This is in a nation of 342 million. So, the density of vehicle ownership in the USA is very high. This puts enormous pressure on road infrastructure, the maintenance of which is getting more costly. The vehicles on the roads of the USA use an average of 376 million gallons of fuel per day. This is an enormous rate of consumption, which comes around costing all drivers more. 98% of Americans travel by car every day. On average, forty-one miles are driven per person per day in the pursuit of work, leisure, and other driving pursuits. In fact, there is a cliché that says, "no car, no job, no American dream." New car prices have risen by 31% between 2000 and 2024. Used car prices have risen by 40%. Auto insurance costs risen by 14% within the same period. All costs are projected to be higher. As we can see, the role of applying common sense to our driving habits is essential in this day and age.

Fender-Bender-Mender Costs

When a fender-bender happens, whom are you going to call? It is the fender-bender mender, who comes at an increasingly higher cost in the modern digital-leaning society. Most vehicles today are increasingly computerized. A simple mending of fenders is no longer the rule of the day. Nowadays, replacing a part of a vehicle may require replacing several digital components as well, thereby increasing the overall cost of vehicle repairs.

WRECK AND ENERGY TRANSFER

Energy is, indeed, a fascinating topic both from intellectual and usage standpoints. Even if, as engineers, we are already versed in the science of energy, new reinforcement in the social context of the present energy crisis will be informative. We must understand the inherent scientific characteristics of energy to fully appreciate the perilous future that we face if we don't act now. There are two basic forms of energy:

- **Kinetic Energy**
- **Potential Energy**

All other forms of energy are derived from the above two fundamental forms. Energy that is stored (i.e., not being used) is potential energy. Energy transfer research enables us to understand how energy goes from one form to another. In car wrecks, energy is transferred from one form to another and from one object to another.

Kinetic energy is found in anything that is in motion (e.g., waves, electrons, atoms, molecules, and physical objects). Anything that moves produces kinetic energy, but what makes it move requires its own source of energy. Electrical energy is the movement of electrical charges. Radiant energy is electromagnetic energy traveling in waves. Radiant energy includes light, X-rays, gamma rays, and radio waves. Solar energy is an example of radiant energy. Motion energy is the movement of objects and substances from one place to another. Wind is an example of motion energy. Thermal or heat energy is the vibration and movement of matter (atoms and molecules inside a substance). Sound is a form of energy that moves in waves through a material. Sound is produced when a force causes an object to vibrate. The perception of sound is the sensing (picking up) of the vibration of an object.

Potential energy represents energy content by virtue of gravitational position as well as stored energy. For example, energy caused by fuel, food, and elevation (gravity) represents potential energy. Chemical energy is energy derived from atoms and molecules contained in materials. Petroleum and natural gas are examples of chemical energy. Mechanical energy is the energy stored in a material by the application of force. Compressed springs and stretched rubber bands are examples of stored mechanical energy. Nuclear energy is stored in the nucleus of an atom. Gravitational energy is the energy of position and place. Water retained behind the wall of a dam is a demonstration of gravitational potential energy. Light is a form of energy that travels in waves. The light we see is referred to as visible light. However, there is also an invisible spectrum. Infrared or ultraviolet rays cannot be seen but can be felt as heat. Sunburn is an example of the effect of infrared energy on the skin. The difference between visible and invisible light is the length of the radiation wave, known as wavelengths. Radio waves have the longest rays while gamma rays have the shortest rays.

The mass of an object is an inherent property that conveys the amount of matter contained in the object. Mass is a fundamental property that is hard to define in terms of something else. Any physical quantities can be defined in terms of mass, length, and time. Mass is normally considered to be an unchanging property of an object. The usual symbol for mass is m and its SI unit is the kilogram.

The weight of an object is the force of gravity on it and may be defined as the mass times the acceleration of gravity, as shown below:

weight = mass x acceleration due to gravity

Since the weight is a force, its SI unit is the Newton. Density is defined as:

Density = mass/volume

When we ordinarily talk about conserving energy, we often refer to reducing our consumption to save energy. Recalling Newton's law, energy cannot be created or destroyed. When energy is used, it does not disappear; it simply goes from one form to another. For example, solar energy cells change radiant energy into electrical energy. As an automobile engine burns gasoline (a form of chemical energy), it is transformed from the chemical form to a mechanical form. When energy is converted from one form to another, a useful portion of it is always lost because no conversion process is perfectly efficient. It is the objective of energy engineers to minimize that loss by putting the loss into another useful form. Therein lies the need to use Industrial Engineering and Operations Research techniques to mathematically model the interaction of variables in an energy system to achieve an optimized combination of energy resources for energy requirement of products, particularly new products.

It is a physical fact that there is abundant energy in the world. It is just a matter of meeting technical requirements to convert it into useful and manageable forms; from one source to another. For example, the sun converts 600 million tons of hydrogen into 596 million tons of helium through nuclear fusion every second. The remaining 4 million tons of hydrogen is converted into energy in accordance with Einstein's Theory of Relativity, which famously states that:

$$E = mc^2,$$

E represents energy, *m* represents mass of matter, and *c* represents the speed of light. This equation says that energy and mass are equivalent and transmutable. That is, they are fundamentally the same thing. The equation confirms that a very large amount of energy can be released quickly from an extremely small amount of matter. This is why atomic weapons are so powerful and effective. The Theory of Relativity is also the basic principle behind the sun converting matter into energy. The sun produces a large amount of energy that equates to 40,000 watts per square inch on the visible surface of the sun. This can be effectively harnessed for use on Earth and it accounts for the ongoing push to install more solar systems to meet our energy needs.

Although the Earth receives only one-half of a billionth of the sun's energy, this still offers sufficient potential for harnessing. Comprehensive technical, quantitative, and qualitative analysis will be required to achieve widespread harnessing around the world. Industrial Engineering and Operations Research can play an important role in that energy pursuit. The future of energy will involve several integrative decisions involving technical and managerial issues such as:

- Point-of-Use generation.
- Co-generation systems.
- Micro-power generation systems.

- Energy supply transitions.
- Coordination of energy alternatives.
- Global energy competition.
- Green-power generation systems.
- Integrative harnessing of sun, wind, and water energy sources.
- Energy generation, transformation, transmission, distribution, storage, and consumption across global boundaries.
- Sociallyresponsible Megawatt systems (i.e., to invest in reducing electricity demand instead of investing to increase electricity generation capacity).

All the above details about energy are important for driving safety, just as they are for all other human pursuits. If drivers appreciate these details, they will be socially responsible consumers of energy and users of the road systems. Even the minuscule issue of conserving energy while driving has long-term implications in the overall scheme of our existence.

The Inclined Plane

An inclined plane is a surface set at a horizontal angle and used to raise objects that are too heavy to lift vertically. Often referred to as a ramp, the inclined plane allows us to multiply the applied force over a longer distance. In other words, we exert less force for a longer distance. The same amount of work is done, but it just seems easier because it is spread over time.

If an object is placed on an inclined plane it will move if the force of friction is smaller than the combined force of gravity and normal force. If the angle of the inclined plane is 90 degrees (rectangle) the object will free fall.

For example, in soccer ball juggling, for example, a skillful player can use his or her outstretched leg and thigh as a ramp to roll the ball down (as shown below) onto his or her foot before flipping the ball into a juggling routine. Below is an illustration of a leg and thigh in an inclined plane posture.

The Wedge

A wedge works in a similar way to the inclined plane, however it is forced into an object to prevent it from moving or to split it into pieces. A knife is a common use of the wedge. Other examples are axes, forks, nails, and door wedges.

The wedge is a modification of the inclined plane. The mechanical advantage of a wedge can be found by dividing the length of either slope by the thickness of the longer end. In the illustration below, the tip of the soccer shoe is used as a wedge to separate the ball from the ground; thereby lifting the ball up for further skillful handling. As with the inclined plane, the mechanical advantage gained by using a wedge requires a corresponding increase in distance.

Soccer is a game of constant motion and energy dissipation. In sports, a player must be in shape and be capable of always moving while on the field. Even if they don't have the ball, the movements of a player can still play (pun intended) a significant role in what happens on other parts of the field.

The principles of physics are crucial in understanding the characteristics of a body in motion, be it the soccer ball, a player's body, or a car's infrastructure.

Mechanics deals with the relations of force, matter, and motion. This chapter deals with the mathematical methods of describing motion. This computational branch of mechanics is called *kinematics*. Motion is defined as a continuous change of position. In most actual motions, different points in a body move along different paths. The complete motion is known if we know how each point in the body moves. We can consider only a moving point in a body, or a very small body called a *particle*.

The position of a particle is specified by its projections onto the three axes of a rectangular coordinate system. As the particle moves along any path in space, its projections move in straight lines along the three axes. The actual motion can be reconstructed from the motions of these three projections. For example, accident reconstruction exercises make use of object motion analysis.

If we consider a particle moving along the x-axis, we can plot its x coordinate as a function of time, t. The displacement of a particle as it moves from one point of its path to another is defined as the vector Δx drawn from the first point to the second point. Thus, the vector from P to Q, of magnitude $x_2 - x_1 = \Delta x$, is the displacement. The *average velocity* of the particle is then defined as the ratio of the displacement to the time interval $t_2 - t_1 = \Delta t$. The purpose here is not to overwhelm the reader with intricate details of kinematics; but rather to pique the interest of young readers in understanding that there is some scientific principle behind what happens on the soccer playing fields. More advanced readers can consult regular Physics textbooks to get the computational details at whatever level the reader desires.

Based on the foregoing discussions, the reader can now better appreciate the relationships between a car's mass, movement, mobility, agility, and ability to exhibit collision avoidance. Fender-to-fender contact can be unnerving in a wreck. The laws of motion and energy transfer are essential in understanding all road processes. Consider the accident report below, which highlights how energy could be transferred to cause a disastrous outcome.

Two people were killed and at least one person injured late Monday morning on Interstate 75 after a wheel came off a semi tractor-trailer. A van was struck by the wheel at 11 a.m. on I-75 North at the sixty-six mile marker, just inside Miami County from Montgomery County, according to the Ohio State Highway Patrol's Dayton Post. Two people were pronounced dead at the scene and at least one person was taken to a local hospital. Another vehicle reportedly was involved in the crash on the northbound lanes. Source: Dayton Daily News.

This is a sad case of energy transferred from one object to another. The human body, unfortunately, could not absorb or dissipate the energy transferred. Thus, leading to an unpleasant outcome.

DEJI'S TIPS FOR SAFE DRIVING

In this concluding section, I present a collection of tips, concepts, aphorisms, wisecracks, guidelines, and practices to encourage paying more attention in the pursuit of safe driving. If we all want to go wreckless in the city and beyond, we must imbibe new approaches to our driving habits. My own habits have helped my driving cleanliness for over 50 years. Other drivers should aim to drive likewise.

- **Avoid the Moth Effect.** The Moth Effect is one cause of nighttime driving collisions. The Moth Effect theory suggests that many nighttime collisions occur when drivers are attracted to or mesmerized by lights in the dark. This is similar to the way moths are drawn to a flame. Drivers are susceptible to the glare from vehicle lights. For this reason, be extra careful with night driving, if night driving must be done at all.

- **Avoid target fixation**. Target fixation is a behavior in which a person becomes so focused on a singular object that they tend to ride (or drive) straight into it. The term was first used during World War II to describe fighter pilots who flew into the very targets they were strafing. This occurs more commonly in motorcyclists because the steering on a motorcycle is much more attuned to the miniscule, sometimes-subconscious, movements of the rider.
- **Avoid perceptual tropism**: This is a reactionary behavior related to the perceptual significance of the oncoming vehicle. This behavior was more pronounced on narrow roads than wide roads and is not affected by driving experience.
- Observe and obey all road signs, signals, and alerts. They are posted for a reason.
- "If you want to get there fast, you should leave earlier." – Deji Badiru
- "Wherever you are going, you can get there at the speed limit." – Deji Badiru
- "If there is no coincidence, there is no story." Chinese saying.
- If you don't have to drive, don't drive.
- Remember, drinking and driving don't mix.
- For the right-hand-side driving system, never overtake from the right side. You cannot see what is speeding up on the other side. The reverse is true for the left-hand-side driving system.

- NEVER, NEVER, NEVER follow too closely. Most accidents are caused by drivers following too closely and unable to react to events unfolding rapidly in front.
- Speeding won't get you there faster because there is a risk of not getting there at all.
- Never cut sharply in front of other vehicles. You can never anticipate how the other driver might react.
- Natural laws: Respect and observe the natural laws of gravity and friction when driving.
- General laws: Observe and extend the general social laws of obedience and sacrifice. Obedience in the sense of obeying laws of the road. Sacrifice in the sense of not using up all the allowable speed limit on a fast road.
- Spiritual laws: Demonstrate kindness and forgiveness on the roads. No one is perfect. Other drivers may rely on and benefit from your own goodwill for both of you to avoid a collision.
- Maintain your vehicle to keep it in the best shape possible. Changing the oil regularly is one of the easiest things to do to keep your vehicle operating superbly.
- Ensure you have sufficient fuel in your vehicle. Putting gas in the tank when needed is the best way to avoid roadside disasters. Vehicles that are stuck on the side of the road have accounted for run-in roadside accidents.

- Road rage: Avoid road-rage entanglements. Road-rage flare-ups create ever-present problems on city roadways.
- Put down your phone.
- Please, please, please, text later.
- Get out of the passing lane and let passers pass.
- Wear your seat belt.
- By all means, focus on the road when you drive.
- Practice accident avoidance every time. Don't trust the other drivers. Be proactive. Take control of avoiding accidents.

Printed in the United States
by Baker & Taylor Publisher Services